James Challis

A Translation of the Epistle of the Apostle Paul to the Romans

James Challis

A Translation of the Epistle of the Apostle Paul to the Romans

ISBN/EAN: 9783744696630

Printed in Europe, USA, Canada, Australia, Japan

Cover: Foto ©Lupo / pixelio.de

More available books at **www.hansebooks.com**

THE EPISTLE OF THE APOSTLE PAUL

TO

THE ROMANS.

A TRANSLATION

OF THE

EPISTLE OF THE APOSTLE PAUL

TO

THE ROMANS,

WITH AN INTRODUCTION AND CRITICAL NOTES.

BY THE

REV. JAMES CHALLIS, M.A., F.R.S., F.R.A.S.,

PLUMIAN PROFESSOR OF ASTRONOMY AND EXPERIMENTAL PHILOSOPHY IN
THE UNIVERSITY OF CAMBRIDGE, AND FELLOW OF TRINITY COLLEGE.

Τὰ γὰρ ἀόρατα αὐτοῦ ἀπὸ κτίσεως κόσμου, τοῖς ποιήμασι νοούμενα, καθορᾶται, ἥ τε ἀΐδιος αὐτοῦ δύναμις καὶ θειότης. Rom. i. 20.

CAMBRIDGE:
DEIGHTON, BELL, AND CO.
LONDON: BELL AND DALDY.
1871.

[All Rights reserved.]

PREFACE.

ANY one who undertakes to write on a subject for the treatment of which he may be supposed to be unprepared, by reason of a preoccupation of his time and thoughts in another direction, must expect that the undertaking will be generally regarded with distrust, and that the execution of it will be closely criticized by those whose province he may seem to invade. Feeling this to be my case in publishing, after the devotion of many years of my life to mathematics and physical science, a Translation, with annotations, of the Epistle of St Paul to the Romans,—perhaps the most difficult portion of the New Testament,—I beg, in order to extenuate the presumption with which I may appear to be chargeable, to submit the following statement of the circumstances under which I have been induced to prosecute the work, and my reasons for publishing it at this juncture.

My attention was first directed specially to the Greek of the New Testament in the year 1823, when I was an undergraduate of Trinity College. It was the custom of the College to set one of the Gospels, or the Acts of the Apostles, as a subject for the reading of men of the second year, although the Previous Examination had not at that time been instituted. The Gospel of St Luke was

b

selected for the year 1823, and I attended lectures upon it by Julius Charles Hare, and was examined in it by Mr (afterwards Professor) Scholefield. The examination paper contained the following question: "What is the nature of the difference between the language of classical Greek writers, and that of the authors of the New Testament? Will this difference justify the supposition of an *arbitrary* use or neglect of the article? State the most remarkable cases of either the omission or insertion of the article; and illustrate them by examples from the New Testament." It happened that by a change of plan, first adopted in 1824, the Acts of the Apostles was set as a subject for the third year men, so that I had the advantage of two examinations in books of the New Testament. I ascribe it to the interest excited by these examinations and the preparations for them, that I subsequently devoted much attention to the critical study of the New Testament, with respect both to philological questions, such as those contained in the above quotation from one of the examination papers, and to the doctrinal bearing of correct principles of interpretation. The study was carried on in the midst of engagements of a very different kind, until, after having given particular attention to the Epistle of St Paul to the Romans, I made preparations in 1833 for publishing "Remarks critical and explanatory on some passages of that Epistle;" and in the Cambridge Calendars of 1833 and 1834 may be seen advertisements to that effect. Two sheets were actually printed at the University Press: but demands on my time arising from clerical duty and giving instruction to house pupils, and subsequently my appointment to the superintendence of the Cambridge Observatory in the early part of 1836, compelled a suspension, and eventually an abandonment of the work.

PREFACE.

In the long interval between 1836 and the present year the intention of publishing my views on the Epistle to the Romans was at no time given up, and I continued at all available opportunities to devote attention to the critical study both of that Epistle and of other Books of the New Testament. In order to acquire familiarity with the diction, and to impress passages on my memory, I made it a rule always to have the Greek Testament within reach, taking with me in travelling the small edition of Griesbach's Recension, published by Rivingtons in 1829, which contains the more important various readings. In the same interval also, a vast amount of critical apparatus has been collected and published by biblicists, by means of which I have been enabled to take up the work with greatly increased advantages; and while my views on some critical points of grammar and interpretation have undergone correction, on others they have been confirmed, or enlarged. On these various accounts I have no reason to regret that the project has been so tardily accomplished. So much of the results of my labors in 1833 as I could now approve of, I have incorporated into the present publication.

The foregoing details, some of which will perhaps be thought to be trivial and of too personal a character, have been stated, first, with the object of shewing that I have not inconsiderately entered upon this arduous task, nor without due preparation; and, again, to put on record my sense of the advantage I, in common with many others, possess in having learnt, by means of the Cambridge system of teaching Classics, how to translate Greek, and, in particular, the Greek of the New Testament, with *precision*. So great do I consider this advantage that I am glad to see the means of partaking of it within reach of all denominations of my fellow-countrymen.

For the same reason also I think it is much to be deprecated that any measure should be adopted in this University which might have the effect of diminishing the inducement to study the original of the New Testament, and causing such study to be less attended to in the public schools.

My reason for publishing at this time has arisen out of the scheme recently set on foot by Convocation for revising, by the labours of two companies, the Authorized Version of the Old and New Testaments. Respecting the Revision of the Old Testament I have nothing to say. But as far as I have been able to judge from publications which may be supposed to give some idea of what may be expected from the company of Revisers of the New Testament, it appeared to me that qualifications were needed which are not usually possessed by those whose intellectual training has been exclusively *classical*. The publications I refer to are the Revisions of the Gospel of St John and of six of St Paul's Epistles by "Five Clergymen," a Revision of the whole of the New Testament by Alford, incorporating those just mentioned, and recent publications on the Revision of the New Testament by Bishop Ellicott and Professor Lightfoot. In these works I seem also to see (1) the want of a due appreciation of the principles and exigencies of language *in general*, especially of the language of ordinary intercourse, such as that in which the New Testament was written may be supposed to have been; (2) a too technical application of grammatical rules for which *classical writers* alone are referred to as standards; (3) evidence of want of critical acquaintance with the Greek of the Septuagint, which has much in common with the Greek of the New Testament. How far I have sustained these indictments I leave to be judged of by what is said in the Introduction and in the Notes. I have canvassed very freely many of the translations proposed in the above-mentioned works, thinking that in a matter of so great importance as a translation of the Scriptures, forbearing from personal considerations to criticize unreservedly would be wholly out of place. I desire the same measure to be dealt to my efforts; and I cannot but think that the body of revisers will wish the result of their labours, when finally produced, to be submitted to the severest scrutiny. In order to give some intimation before publishing this work of my views respecting the Revision of the New Testament, I made a communication on the subject to the *Guardian*, but the Editor did not insert the letter.

That in the publications I have referred to a large number of good alterations are proposed may be readily admitted. But it would appear that this is not much to say; for the great difficulty revisers in general have to contend with is, to avoid altering what needs no alteration. Although personally I should not feel any hesitation in introducing the slightest change which I considered to be an improvement, I have yet had occasion, as will be seen from the Notes, to defend the Authorized Version in many instances from changes proposed by the revisers which I judged to be either needless or erroneous. Whether I have done so rightly or wrongly, the judgment has at least not been influenced by any unreasonable scruple about making changes.

It will be seen that I have discarded the (now) archaic form of the Authorized Version, and made the experiment of translating into the current English of the day. This course is defended by reasons given in the Introduction.

PREFACE.

But the main feature of this work, which, perhaps, might alone be considered to justify its publication is, that it recognizes in St Paul's Epistle a use of the word 'law' with respect to a spiritual creation in precisely the sense in which we have been led by the pursuit of physical science to employ it with respect to the natural creation. The Apostolic sense of the word is best understood by its scientific sense. The great significance of this fact will be seen by considering that during many centuries the doctrine of St Paul (as also that of other parts of Scripture) could not have been as fully comprehended as by the Providence of God we may be enabled to comprehend it in the present day. Much light is thrown by this theory on the principles of the Apostle's reasoning in the doctrinal parts; and on account of the necessary connection between translation and interpretation, the character of the translation is also thereby in great measure determined. It is on this ground mainly that the translation lays claim to the consideration of Biblical students. These views will be found to be sustained by argument at the end of the Introduction and in the Notes. Thus my devotion to physical enquiries, which, as I said above, might be thought to be a disqualification for the task I have undertaken, has really proved to have an important bearing on the successful execution of it, and made it a kind of duty on my part to place before my fellow Christians this result of my labors.

CAMBRIDGE,
June 1, 1871.

INTRODUCTION.

THE translation of St Paul's Epistle to the Romans which I venture to offer for the consideration of Biblical scholars, and of my English-speaking fellow-Christians in general, was committed to writing, together with the Notes appended to it, in an interleaved copy of Scholz's edition (1836) of the New Testament, and for the most part just as it is now published. Consequently, although I have not adopted the text of that edition, I have taken advantage of its collation with the Alexandrine and Received Texts, and of the numerous various readings, and references to MSS. and ancient authorities, which are contained in it. I have, besides, had before me the "Novum Testamentum Græce" published by Tischendorf in 1859 (which in its critical apparatus includes Lachmann's recension), and also that published by the same editor in 1865 from the Codex Sinaiticus, respecting the genuineness and antiquity of which MS. I never had any doubt. Alford's Greek Testament (ed. 1865) has been perpetually consulted, as well with regard to the various readings and the text, as to the annotations. In the course of translating I frequently turned, for comparison, to Jerome's Latin Version, which, as it seemed to me, had no inconsiderable influence upon the character of the English Authorized Version, as far, at least, as regards the Epistle to the Romans. In citing Jerome's Version I have referred to the edition published by Tischendorf in 1850 from the Codex Amiatinus.

The foregoing brief notices may suffice to shew that I have not neglected to avail myself of the materials which have been collected by modern biblicists for obtaining a correct text of the New Testament. I did not, however, consider it to be necessary for my purpose to exhibit a text in full, and accordingly I have limited myself to giving intimations in the Notes of readings specially adopted, together with the reasons for preferring them. The text as a whole might, if thought desirable, be inferred in all essential respects from the translation itself. It would, I think, be thus found that I have followed pretty closely the text of Alford.

But it has appeared to me, for reasons that will be fully stated in the sequel of this Introduction, that with the exception of a very limited number of passages in the New Testament, the exact text is of much less importance, as respects the determination of the true sense of the original, than correct grammatical principles of translation combined with correct principles of interpretation. I propose therefore, to exhibit here as distinctly as possible the principles both of translation and interpretation (for the two things cannot be dissociated), on which the present translation has been made, especially where they have led to renderings of the Greek differing from those that have been hitherto admitted. The points that will come under discussion relate chiefly to *the usage of the Greek article*, and to the translation of Greek *tenses*, especially the *aorist* and the *perfect*.

It will be proper to make the preliminary statement that I have all along carefully compared my translation both with the Authorized Version and with the Revision of the Authorized Version by Five Clergymen, published in 1858; and that, consequently, when I do not agree with that Revision, it is either because I deliberately concluded that its deviations from the Authorized Version were needless or erroneous, or that corrections had not been made where they were required. These cases are taken into consideration, either expressly or implicitly, in the Notes. The numerous cases of accordance with the corrections of the Revisers have not often called for remark, the majority being such as would be generally agreed upon by biblical scholars of the present day.

The usage of the Greek Article.

In various languages, as is well known, a use of the definite article prevails which the idiom of the English language rejects. For instance ἡ ἀρετή in Greek, la vertu in French, die Tugend in German, la virtu in Italian, &c., when taken in an abstract sense, is expressed in English by 'virtue' without the article, just as in Latin by *virtus*. We could not give to '*the* virtue' the same abstract signification. The languages which have this use of the article (which for distinction I shall call *abstract*) employ it also in the ordinary indicative or demonstrative sense with which we are familiar in English. Latin has neither usage, excepting that *ille* occurs occasionally as an indicative article.

Several languages also, as French, German, Italian, &c., agree with English in the use of the so-called indefinite article 'a' or 'an,' which, however, does not occur either in Greek or Latin. Lastly, in those languages which admit the abstract article, nouns are often employed without having the definite article prefixed, in accordance with Latin and English usage. These diversities respecting the use of the article in different languages are here stated, because it is conceived that the reasons that can be assigned for them may assist in laying down rules for the translation of the Greek article into English. These reasons appear to me to be such as follows.

There can be little doubt that the primitive use of the article was simply *indicative*, corresponding to that of the Latin demonstrative pronoun *ille*. At first ἡ ἀρετή was the brave act of a warrior, ἡ ἁμαρτία was the missing of a mark, &c.; that is, in each case some object or event actually witnessed was indicated by the article, and the noun had a concrete signification. In our own language we are accustomed to say the sun, the stars, the earth, &c., these being objects which are continually before us and may be *pointed at with the finger*. When the concrete nouns subsequently acquired a more abstract signification, it depended wholly on national characteristics and modes of thought, (with which language is indissolubly connected), as to whether the article was retained or dropped. In English the absence of the definite article gives to the noun (proper names being excepted) an abstract or general signification; in Latin the same circumstance *allows of* such significations. In Greek, French, &c., the retention of the definite article either indicates, or does not *exclude*, an abstract or general sense, although in this use of it the article seems scarcely to answer any other purpose than shewing the necessary dependence of an abstract idea upon an antecedent concrete one. Perhaps this law of thought accounts for the retention.

The following example will serve to illustrate some of the foregoing remarks. In Rom. v. 3, 4, we read ἡ θλίψις ὑπομονὴν κατεργάζεται, ἡ δὲ ὑπομονὴ δοκιμήν, ἡ δὲ δοκιμὴ ἐλπίδα, which in English is, 'tribulation works patience, and patience experience, and experience hope,' and in French, as given in Ostervald's New Testament, 'l'affliction produit la patience, et la patience l'épreuve, et l'épreuve l'espérance.' Here, where all the nouns are used abstractedly, French has six articles, Greek has three, and English (as also Latin) admits of none. It is remarkable that in this instance Greek approaches more nearly than modern French to the Latin usage.

INTRODUCTION.

But English, in common with Greek, French, German, &c., has the ordinary indicative use of the definite article, while Latin has not. How, it may be asked, can Latin dispense with it? This question admits, I think, of the following explicit answer. What the definite article in this use of it points at, or refers to, may always in correct composition be gathered from the *immediate* context, or from indicated circumstances. When the circumstances under which Pilate spoke, and the force of *ecce*, are considered, 'Ecce homo,' is quite as definite as either Ἴδε ὁ ἄνθρωπος, or, 'Behold the man,' notwithstanding the absence of the definite article. In John xx. 15, Jerome's *hortulanus* may be considered to be equivalent to ὁ κηπουρὸς, 'the gardener,' because it had been before stated that the sepulchre was in a garden. And so in other instances. Hence it may be concluded that the use of the definite article for indication or reference, although it facilitates the understanding of the composition, is not indispensable. Analogous considerations are applicable to the absence of the *indefinite* article in Latin, inasmuch as recorded circumstances and the immediate context determine in like manner in what cases it has to be supplied in translating into English. On these principles it is possible to account for the fact that Latin, although it has no article, is capable of answering all the purposes of a language. It would be marvellous indeed if a language which was for so long a time in general use were not of this character.

Again, Greek has no indefinite article, and consequently it sometimes becomes necessary to decide, in case the noun has no article, whether in translating into English the indefinite article is to be supplied. This determination requires generally the same considerations as those applicable to Latin composition. But there is, besides, a rule of considerable importance which must also be taken into account, viz. *that the Greek definite article is sometimes equivalent to an indefinite article.* I shall presently endeavour to prove by citing examples that this rule is true (at least in Biblical Greek), although I am aware that Bishop Ellicott, on the authority of Hermann, has asserted the contrary in his recent publication on the Revision of the English New Testament (note in p. 132).

Lastly, in many instances in which a Greek noun occurs without an article, we have to determine, in translating into English, whether it should have no article, or the definite article, or the indefinite article. This determination is to be made according to rules and principles applicable to the translating of *Latin* into English. The omission of

INTRODUCTION. xv

the article is very frequent in the New Testament, especially in some of St Paul's Epistles. It is still more frequent in the Septuagint, in parts of which the usage as respects the article approaches very closely to that of Latin.

The foregoing general principles point to the following simple rule for rendering the Greek article in English:—Enquire, first, whether the narrative or context shews that it must be rendered by the English definite article; if not, whether it is shewn by the narrative or context to be equivalent to the English indefinite article; if it is translatable by neither of these, it is the abstract article, and requires that the noun to which it is prefixed should be without an article in the English. I proceed next to adduce examples of the application of this rule.

Alford translates 1 Tim. iv. 13, 'Till I come, give attention to the reading, to the exhortation, to the doctrine.' But the context does not enable us to answer the questions, what reading? what exhortation? what doctrine? Consequently the articles are not indicative. It is obvious that they cannot be indefinite articles. Hence, by the rule, they are abstract articles, and not translatable into English; so that the A. V. is here right. The adoption of the alterations seems to have arisen from not recognizing the abstract force of the Greek article.

Alford and Ellicott both translate Matth. v. 1, 'and seeing the multitudes he went up into the mountain' (εἰς τὸ ὄρος). It had just before been said that "Jesus went about all Galilee" and great multitudes from distant regions followed him (iv. 25); but neither the name, nor the locality, of any mountain was mentioned. Hence the article cannot be used here indicatively. Dr Ellicott has shewn (in the work already cited, p. 132) that it has not an abstract, or generic sense, so as to signify "mountain-country." Hence by exhaustion, according to the above rule, this is an indefinite article, and the translation, 'a mountain,' of the A. V. is correct. It may be remarked that the Greek article, in this use of it, points indefinitely to an *individual of a class;* but does not specify the individual. It individualizes, but does not particularize.

On the same principle ἐν τῷ πλοίῳ in Matth. iv. 21 is rightly translated 'in a ship,' this being the first mention of a ship, and nothing in the context specifying a particular one. However probable it may be that the sons of Zebedee followed their occupation in a particular ship, the rules of intelligible writing demanded a previous statement of this circumstance, if it was intended that ἐν τῷ πλοίῳ should be taken to mean 'in that ship.' No mere presumption, however strong, is grammatically a justification of the use in this instance of the indicative definite article. (The same remark applies to the translation of τὸ ὄρος spoken of above.) In verse 22, τὸ πλοῖον is 'the ship,' because mention had been before made of a ship.

In Matth. v. 15, 'a bushel,' 'a candlestick,' need not be altered, because, as it cannot be gathered from the context that a particular bushel or candlestick is meant, the articles are not indicative, but merely individualize. The substitution of definite articles would convey to the English reader a special sense different from that in which the passage would be understood by a Greek, which is rather given by the indefinite articles. In Joh. xii. 24 our idiom would allow of translating ὁ κόκκος τοῦ σίτου 'the grain of wheat;' but there the Revisers have retained 'a grain.'

The same rule decides, that in a very important passage, Matth. i. 23, ἡ παρθένος should be translated 'a virgin,' the prophecy not pointing to a particular virgin, but specially to the *virginity* of the mother. 'One who is a virgin shall conceive, &c.'[1] It is wholly unreasonable to cite with reference to this point a *following* passage (Is. viii. 1—4), where certainly no mention is made of a virgin. This is a highly figurative passage, the interpretation of which appears to be, that by union with a prophetess (τὴν προφῆτιν), that is, by partaking of the prophetic spirit, Isaiah was enabled to foretell, respecting that same son of the virgin, that he was destined from the beginning to be the spoil-taker, who should lead captivity captive, and therefore be more potent than the king of Assyria, or any earthly king.

The Translation 'through the patience and the comfort of the Scriptures' (Rom. xv. 4), proposed by the "Five Clergymen," is proved to be incorrect by the fact that in the most trustworthy MSS., including the Codex Sinaiticus, the preposition διὰ is repeated before τῆς παρακλήσεως. According to a rule given in a note in p. 76 of the work by Bishop Ellicott already cited, the translation should be 'through patience, and through comfort of the Scriptures.' The next preceding verse shews that patience is here spoken of in a sense independent of the subsequent mention of the Scriptures, and there is no need of the article before 'comfort,' because the character of the comfort is defined by 'of the Scriptures' following. In the Collect for the second Sunday in Advent there is a comma after 'patience.'

The non-recognition by the Revisers of the abstract use of the

---

[1] Luther translates, *eine Jungfrau*, Ostervald, *une vierge*. The Italian version of Antonio Martini has *la Vergine*, probably for a doctrinal reason.

article is still more shewn by the translation 'we might have our hope' at the end of the same passage (Rom. xv. 4). There is no word in the original corresponding to 'our,' which is apparently introduced only because 'our hope' might also be expressed in English by 'the hope of us,' and thus the possessive pronoun gives a sort of reason for taking the article before 'hope' in an indicative rather than an abstract sense. The Revision is disfigured by many other instances of insertions of the possessive pronoun on the same principle. How untenable this principle is will become apparent by comparing the revised translation of the passage before us with that of Rom. v. 3, 4, which contains the same doctrine respecting the generation of hope through patience. Here the Revisers have given, 'tribulation worketh endurance [i.e. patience], and endurance approval, and approval hope,' thus taking, as it were of necessity, all the articles as abstract, and all the nouns, inclusive of 'hope,' in a perfectly general sense. There is, it is true, an instance of a similar insertion of the possessive pronoun in Heb. xii. 2, according to the Authorized Version, where τῆς πίστεως is translated 'of our faith,' the word 'our' being put in Italics as not being in the original. Alford in his revised New Testament, has 'of the faith.' Both these translations, in consequence of not recognizing the abstract force of the article, tend to obscure the doctrine that Jesus Christ is "the author and finisher of faith" generally, that is, of the faith of all the faithful of all times.

As the definite article is used in the French language just as in Greek to give to a noun an abstract sense, it might be argued that, according to the laws of language, if it has a pronominal force in Greek, it has the same in French. But this, I suppose, Frenchmen would not admit. In short, I venture to express the opinion that the so-called pronominal force of the Greek article is a *fiction*, referable to no linguistic principle, and originating partly in a too technical application of Middleton's doctrine of the article, and partly in the tendency, characteristic of modern biblical criticism, to give to the language of Scripture a concrete or objective sense.

Translation of Greek Tenses.

Although we have tenses in English corresponding to the present, the imperfect, the aorist, the perfect and the pluperfect, in Greek, it is not always required, neither is it always possible, to translate these tenses by the corresponding ones in English. Yet the variations should be such as may be accounted for on linguistic principles.

I propose, therefore, to enquire what are the principles which in certain cases justify translating a Greek tense by a different English one, with the view of ascertaining rules for guidance in such cases with respect to translating the tenses in the Greek of the New Testament.

In the Authorized Version, Joh. iv. 1 and 2 is translated, 'When, therefore, the Lord knew how the Pharisees had heard that Jesus made and baptized more disciples than John, (though Jesus himself baptized not, but his disciples)'. Here the aorist ἤκουσαν is rendered by the pluperfect 'had heard,' the present ποιεῖ by 'made,' and both the present βαπτίζει and the imperfect ἐβάπτιζε by 'baptized;' and these renderings have been retained in the Revision by "Five Clergymen." Excepting that there is an awkwardness in the repetition of the subject Ἰησοῦς after ὁ κύριος, the translated tenses are felt by the reader to be consistent with each other and to give an intelligible account of the transactions narrated. On what principle, then, have the above-mentioned changes been made? I conceive that they are attributable to the circumstance that the translators have stated the course of events with reference to a point of time different from that to which they are referred by the author of the original, and have consequently substituted narrative forms of expression for descriptive. The tenses of the Greek might be exactly rendered by translating as follows: 'When the Lord knew that the Pharisees heard say, Jesus is making and baptizing more disciples than John, although Jesus himself was not baptizing, &c.' The narrative aorist ἤκουσαν is used, because the very terms in which the report was conveyed are added. This will also account for the repetition of the subject above alluded to, and for the descriptive form of the report. The imperfect tense which follows is also descriptive, and implies that at the time the message was brought to the Pharisees the transaction referred to was still going on. On the whole I consider this translation to be preferable to that of A.V., inasmuch as it expresses the Greek tenses more exactly, and at the same time does no violence to English idiom.

In Rom. i. 19, ὁ θεὸς ἐφανέρωσε is rendered in A. V., 'God hath shewed,' which in the present translation is changed into 'God has manifested,' because in the preceding clause the Greek of 'manifest' is φανερόν. The Revisers have given 'God manifested,' translating the aorist strictly. Alford, commenting on the passage, urges that "the historic aorist" is to be adhered to because it accords with the mention made of the Creation in the expression ἀπὸ κτίσεως κόσμου in ver. 20. But this expression, as well as ἀπὸ καταβολῆς κόσμου, is employed solely with reference to the remotest conceivable past *time*,—the very beginning of time,—being equivalent to ἀπ' ἀρχῆς κτίσεως (2 Pet. iii. 4), or to ἀπ' ἀρχῆς κόσμου (Matth. xxiv. 21), or to the simple formula ἀπ' ἀρχῆς (1 Joh. i. 1). (See the Note to Rom. i. 20 in p. 26.) Accordingly ὁ θεὸς ἐφανέρωσε has no special reference to the act of creating the world, but rather to the continual ordering by God of the course of nature and providence so as to reveal Himself to intelligent beings. Such continuous action, or repetition of acts, was resolved in the mental vision of the Greek-speaking people into component parts, which were then severally regarded and spoken of as past events, *whether they were past or future*. Thus the historic aorist is used in the present instance as referring equally to all God's manifestations of Himself. On the contrary, speakers of other languages, as ourselves, would regard the events collectively, and embrace all manifestations by using the perfect past, this tense often referring not only to what has been done, but implicitly also to what is done and will be done. Thus there is actually no difference between the two methods in point of generality, the same general truth being expressed by both, but in more abstract terms in the latter method than in the other. [In an exactly analogous manner, virtue in the abstract is expressed more concretely in Greek by ἡ ἀρετή than in English by 'virtue,' or in Latin by *virtus*.] Some languages, as Latin, do not formally distinguish between the historic past and the perfect past, because, in fact, the distinction may be conveyed by the context and the known circumstances of the narration or the speaker, although it be not actually expressed.

It is, however, very important in translating from one language into another to have regard to the usus loquendi in *each* with respect to tenses. [This is necessary, on account of differences of usage, even in translating from one *modern* language into another.] On this principle, apparently, the translators of the English Version judged that ἐφανέρωσε in the present instance should be rendered by a perfect past. That they judged rightly appears from the circumstance that rendering it by an aorist might lead an English reader to conclude that some particular manifestation, as the act of creation, was referred to; which, as has already been argued, there is no ground for supposing. The foregoing reasons justify, it seems to me, retaining the perfect past tense as given in A. V.

Both in A. V. and in R. A. V. ἥμαρτον in Rom. ii. 12 is translated 'have sinned.' The Revisers assign as the reason for their departure in this instance from the rule they laid down for themselves in translating the aorist, that "there is a prolepsis of the future judgment." This somewhat far-fetched reason, which is inapplicable to other instances of the same translation to be presently mentioned, has, perhaps, had its origin only in the incapacity of modern thought to comprehend the Apostle's abstract language, and may, I think, be set aside by the considerations entered into above in discussing the translation of ἐφανέρωσε. According to those views the aorist ἥμαρτον is really used narratively, but in an abstract general sense, so as to embrace ideally all sinful acts, whether in past, present, or future time. English idiom rejects this usage, but we convey the appropriate idea either by means of the perfect past or the present. I have followed A. V. and R. A. V. in adopting the perfect past in this passage, but I think that the present would express better the meaning of the original. 'As many as sin without law, without law shall also perish, and as many as sin in law through law shall be judged.' (See the Note to ii. 12 in p. 27.) The abstract use of the aorist, if the English mind were trained to it, might tend to render our language more suited to Scriptural reasoning; but as the case is, the adoption of such usage would only mislead.

In A. V. πάντες ἥμαρτον is translated 'all have sinned' both in Rom. iii. 23 and in Rom. v. 12. But R. A. V. has 'all have sinned' in the former passage, and 'all were sinners' in the other. In the latter, Alford gives 'all sinned,' translating the aorist strictly. There can, I think, be no doubt that the translation should be the same in both passages. The last mentioned translation appears to countenance the doctrine that all men sinned in Adam's sin. But if the principles above explained be true, this inference is not justified by the Apostle's language, inasmuch as the aorist is to be taken, not with any such special reference, but as comprehending all individual instances. It is because English readers are generally incapable of so taking 'all sinned,' that the translation 'all have sinned,' which, at least, does not mislead, is preferable. Considering, however, that according to the proposed explanation of the Greek usage, 'all sin' really expresses in English idiom the very same idea as that which was conveyed by πάντες ἥμαρτον to a Greek, the aorist has been rendered by a present in Rom. v. 12, although 'all have sinned' has been allowed to stand in Rom. iii. 23. (See the Note to v. 12 in p. 36.)

On the same principles as those applied to ἥμαρτον, the aorist ἀπεθάνομεν in vi. 2 is translated by a present: 'How shall we who die to sin, &c.' There is the special reason for such rendering in this passage, that, in accordance with the meaning of τὸν θάνατον in ver. 3, it indicates that the death signified is natural death,—that to which the body is subject in consequence of "the law of sin and death" spoken of in viii. 2. (See the Notes to vi. 2 and 3.) The translation in A. V., 'How shall we that are dead to sin, &c.' is not usually supposed to have reference to death of the body, the expression "dead to sin" being vaguely taken in a metaphorical sense. The translation adopted by the "Five Clergymen" is, 'we who died to sin;' but according to Alford's interpretation (*in loc.*), the expression 'died to sin' means, "became as separate from and apathetic towards sin as the dead corpse is separate from and apathetic towards the functions and stir of life." And again in his remarks upon ἁμαρτίας εἰς θάνατον in vi. 16, taking no notice of the law of antecedence of sin to death expressed by this formula, he speaks of "Death [by sin]" as being "the state of misery induced by sin, in all its awful aspects and consequences." I do not hesitate to say that to those who write, and to those who accept, arbitrary comments such as these, the doctrine and the gospel preached by St. Paul are hid, inasmuch as the object of his teaching here is specially to shew, by the light of the death of Christ, to what end sin and death are in the world. Scripture has vouchsafed no other explanation of the existence of evil than that which, according to St Paul's doctrine, is deducible from the death of the Son of God.

For the same reasons ἀπεθάνομεν in vi. 8 and ἀπέθανε in vi. 10 are translated by present tenses. The instances in vi. 10 require particular consideration. In A. V. ὃ ἀπέθανε is translated 'in that he died;' in R. A. V., 'the death that he died.' But both these translations do violence to strict grammar, which demands that the translation should be, 'that which died, died to sin, &c.;' and this being the case, the only question to be determined is, How is this translation to be interpreted? Now I conceive that the answer to this question is given by saying, in reliance upon the foregoing philological principles, that we have in this passage an assertion made *abstractedly* by means of the neuter pronoun ὃ and aorist tenses, and that the very same assertion is made in accordance with English idiom and mode of thought when the aorists are rendered as present tenses:—'That which dies, dies to sin &c.' (See the Note to vi. 10.)

Having explained, as far as may be required, the principles on which the Greek article, and Greek tenses, are rendered in the present Version, I propose to add some miscellaneous remarks on philological points having reference to the exact translation and interpretation not only of St Paul's writings, but of the New Testament generally. One of the most important of these points is *the translation of prepositions*, with respect to which the A. V. in not a few instances requires correction.

I think I have uniformly rendered διά with a genitive, 'through,' or 'by means of,' and διά with an accusative, 'on account of' or 'because of.' In iii. 30 St Paul seems to intimate, by the way in which he uses both ἐκ πίστεως and διὰ πίστεως, that these are equivalent expressions, although differing in form. The difference of form is explainable on the supposition that ἐκ πίστεως expresses the *law* of the relation between faith and righteousness, and διὰ πίστεως the instrumental relation, faith being the *means* of partaking of righteousness. (See the Note to iii. 30.) The mode of using εἰς and ἐπὶ in iii. 22 is another instance indicative of the Apostle's regard to precision with respect to the signification of prepositions.

Generally, the prepositions ἐκ and εἰς are employed to express respectively 'consequence from' and 'antecedence to;' and in such cases the former may be translated 'from,' or 'after,' or 'in consequence of,' and the latter 'unto' or 'into.' (Respecting the translation of εἰς by 'unto', see the Note to x. 3.) The preposition εἰς is in other instances considered to express 'direction towards,' or 'reference to.' In i. 4 ἐκ is taken in the sense of 'because of,' or 'by reason of,' for reasons given in the Note to that passage.

In several instances ἀνάστασις ἐκ τῶν νεκρῶν is translated 'resurrection after death,' οἱ νεκροὶ being considered to be a concrete noun put for the abstract 'death' or 'mortality.' In some instances, however, I have retained 'resurrection from the dead,' this being so established an expression that it cannot now be unsettled, although many who use it have no distinct perception of what is meant by 'from the dead.' Possibly the rendering of ἐκ τῶν νεκρῶν sometimes one way and sometimes the other may serve to suggest to the English reader the meaning of the concrete expression 'from the dead.' (See the Note to vi. 13.)

The preposition ἐκ is often omitted when it governs a noun dependent on another noun. Hermann remarks (on Soph. *Philoct.* l. 3), 'Nemo hodie de omissa prepositione cogitabit, quum genitivus per se indicet id unde quid fiat.' Thus, we have in St Paul's writings δικαι-

INTRODUCTION. xxiii

οσύνη ἐκ πίστεως and δικαιοσύνη πίστεως in nearly the same sense. In the latter form of expression the noun in the genitive case may acquire the force of an adjective. Thus in the present instance the expression might be rendered a faith-righteousness. This genitive, which occurs frequently in the Greek of the New Testament, has been called 'a genitive of quality,' to distinguish it from the ordinary genitive expressive of dependence or relation. In Luke xvi. 9 ἐκ τοῦ μαμωνᾶ τῆς ἀδικίας is an instructive instance, being followed in v. 11 by ἐν τῷ ἀδίκῳ μαμωνᾷ.

I propose next to make a few remarks on the usage in St Paul's writings with respect to the above-mentioned *genitive of quality*. In agreement with R. A. V. I have translated τὴν ἐλευθερίαν τῆς δόξης (Rom. viii. 21) 'the liberty of the glory,' although I am much disposed to conclude that τῆς δόξης is here a genitive of quality, and that 'the glorious liberty' as given in A. V. is a preferable translation. In the latter part of the Note on vii. 24 reasons are given for translating ἐκ τοῦ σώματος τοῦ θανάτου τούτου, 'from this deathful [or mortal] body,' τοῦ θανάτου being taken to be a genitive of quality, and the pronoun τούτου to belong to τοῦ σώματος. This syntax is supported by an instance from the Septuagint. So in Psalm lxxxviii. 10, ἐν τῷ βραχίονι τῆς δυνάμεώς σου is not 'with the arm of thy strength,' but 'with thy arm of strength,' or, as in the English Version, 'with thy strong arm.' According to the same rule, τὸ σῶμα τῆς ταπεινώσεως ἡμῶν in Phil. iii. 21 is 'our body of humiliation,' and τῷ σώματι τῆς δόξης αὐτοῦ in the same verse is 'his body of glory.' These renderings are equivalent to 'our vile body' and 'his glorious body,' as given in A. V. Bishop Ellicott, in his recent work on Revision (p. 109), considers 'the body of our vileness' and 'the body of his glory' to be 'more truthful and forcible' than the expressions in A. V. On the contrary, these renderings (which are given in the Revision of the Epistle to the Philippians published by 'Four Clergymen' in 1861, excepting that 'humiliation' is there in place of 'vileness') appear to me not only incorrect for the reasons above urged, but also unintelligible to the ordinary English reader, because the possessive pronouns are not attached to the word 'body.'

I proceed now to remark upon the translation of *particles*. The rules that have been adopted in this Version in translating the particles μὲν, δὲ, καὶ, οὖν and γάρ call for the following explanations. In the Preface to the Revision of the Gospel of St John by Five Clergymen, the authors remark (p. x.), "the particle δὲ has been variously rendered, according as it seemed to express distinct contrast, or the mere passage from one thing to another, by the words 'but' or 'and'; and in some instances it has been omitted altogether, after the example of the Authorized Version, in cases where the genius of English narrative seemed to call for the lively 'asyndeton,' rather than the continual and linked coherence of the Greek." The rules I have followed with respect to rendering the particle δὲ accord generally with the principles thus laid down, although I do not think that omitting to render it is justified by any difference between the asyndeton character of English narrative and the linked coherence of the Greek. The reason thus assigned leaves out of consideration a very marked distinction between Greek and English writing, viz. the use of *punctuation*, which, whensoever and by whomsoever it was invented, was a great simplification of *written* language. Any one who should attempt to read a piece of English not punctuated, especially if at the same time the words were not separated by spaces, might convince himself that in Greek writing there must have been some equivalent to stops, which served to indicate the transition from one passage or clause to another, and prepared the reader to give to the following one the appropriate tone and emphasis. As the necessities of language are the same in all ages and nations, it may be presumed that that office was discharged by such particles as καὶ, μὲν, δὲ, and οὖν, and the supposition that such was the case will at once account for their holding so generally either the first or second place of a clause or sentence. Probably these particles are representatives of *sounds* used originally in *conversation* for the sake of distinction or emphasis.

As an adversative particle, δὲ is generally equivalent to our 'but'; but as it is not so strongly adversative as ἀλλὰ it may often be rendered 'however,' and sometimes 'yet'. Also as a transitional particle δὲ is always more or less adversative, and in that respect is distinguished from καὶ when the latter is used for transition. Not unfrequently δὲ may be exactly rendered by the English 'now,' used without reference to time, but simply to indicate transition to another phase of the subject.

The particle μὲν is sometimes rendered 'indeed,' not in the sense of 'in reality,' but solely because that word serves, together with punctuation, to guide the reader towards the sense of a passage, just as μὲν does in Greek. Frequently, however, the translation of μὲν is rendered unnecessary by punctuation.

I have, always, I think, rendered γὰρ by 'for,' excepting in the instance of Τί γάρ; in iii. 3, which is translated 'What now?' The usage with respect to this formula is discussed at some length in the Note to that passage, as I could not find anything to the purpose concerning it either in Matthiæ's Grammar, or in Liddell and Scott. I distinguish between ὅτι and γάρ, the former, when it is not equivalent to 'that,' being translated 'because.'

The particle οὖν, when it indicates a general dependence of something preceding on what follows, is translated 'then,' and only in case of a formal inference 'therefore.' Τί οὖν; is 'what then?' Ἆρα οὖν is always 'therefore.'

The uses of the copula καί require to be specially mentioned. Any one acquainted with the language of the Septuagint could not fail to notice the very frequent occurrence of the use of this particle. It seems, in fact, often to be introduced only to separate the clauses of a sentence, and in this respect to answer the same purpose as punctuation. Obviously, one of the uses coming under this category is, *to indicate the commencement of the apodosis of a sentence.* It is surprising to me that this philological fact does not appear to have been noticed by Greek scholars. This is probably to be accounted for by the general neglect into which the diction of the Septuagint seems to have fallen on the part of those who devote their attention to the style and language of classic authors. The following instance of this use of καί occurs in Is. vii. 16: Διότι πρὶν ἢ γνῶναι τὸ παιδίον ἀγαθὸν ἢ κακόν, ἀπειθεῖ πονηρίᾳ, ἐκλέξασθαι τὸ ἀγαθόν· καὶ καταλειφθήσεται ἡ γῆ ἣν σὺ φοβῇ ἀπὸ προσώπου τῶν δύο βασιλέων. [Schleusner in his Lexicon proposes to read ἀπειθεῖν instead of ἀπειθεῖ.] 'For before the child knows good or evil,—to refuse the evil, to choose the good,—the land which thou fearest will be left without the presence of the two kings.' Here καί performs no other office than that of separating the apodosis of the sentence from the antecedent clauses. This use of καί occurs in a similar manner in v. 12 and at the beginning of ix. 23. (See the Notes on those two passages.)

Again, καί is used like δέ for the sake of nexus, but not with any adversative signification. To illustrate this point I propose to advert to the translation of Joh. v. 39, 40, adopted by the "Five Clergymen" in their Revision of the Gospel of St John. They state in the Preface (p. xv.) that they decided, three against two, for the indicative meaning of ἐρευνᾶτε, and accordingly translate, 'Ye search the Scriptures, because ye think that in them ye have eternal life : and they are they which testify of me; and yet ye are not willing to come to me that ye may have life.' If I remember rightly, in a discussion in the House of Lords on a proposed Revision of the Authorized Version, one of the Bishops referred to this passage as exemplifying the great difficulty of deciding unanimously on the translation of disputed passages, and as furnishing a reason for restricting the revision to putting alternative renderings in the margin. But since we may be sure that such passages were understood at the time they were written in the definite meanings intended by the writers, there must exist philological principles by means of which the difficulties that are now felt may be overcome, and it would therefore be unwise to despair of discovering these, as well as inconsistent with the advances in philological science supposed to be made in the present day. At least, with respect to the passage which has given rise to these remarks, I think, for the following reasons, there is no occasion to despair of arriving at a definite and satisfactory result.

The whole passage, inclusive of v. 38, may be thus rendered: 'and ye have not his word abiding in you; for whom he hath sent, him ye believe not. Search the Scriptures, because yourselves think that in them ye have eternal life, and they are they which testify of me. And ye are not willing to come to me that ye may have life.' As ὑμεῖς is expressed before δοκεῖτε, and is evidently put in contrast with ἐκεῖναι following, it should be emphasized; which may be done by translating it 'yourselves.' But for this reason the clause beginning καὶ ἐκεῖναι is dependent on ὅτι, and instead of a colon, only a comma should be put after 'life.' Now our Lord could not say of the Jews he was addressing, who did not believe on him (v. 38), that they searched the Scriptures for testimony concerning himself. Hence the indicative sense of ἐρευνᾶτε is inapplicable. Also the translation of καὶ in v. 40 by 'and yet,' is inadmissible, because it gives to καὶ an adversative sense, which it never has. Rather καὶ is used for nexus, primarily with v. 38, but inclusively with v. 39, as will be seen by paraphrasing this verse as follows: 'Ye do not search the Scriptures, although ye, on your part, think that in them ye have eternal life, and they, on their part, testify of me the Christ; and ye will not come unto me, &c.' Bidding them search the Scriptures because they had good reasons for so doing, is equivalent to saying that they did not search the Scriptures although they had such reasons. This exegesis seems to me to remove all difficulty from the passage.

I take occasion to advert here to a few instances in which, as it seems to me, a species of injustice has been done to the inspired writers, either in consequence of not taking a common-sense view of what they say, or not adequately estimating the character of the writing, or the writer. In Luke ii. 3, ἐπορεύοντο πάντες ἀπογράφεσθαι ought by no means to have been translated 'all went to be taxed,' as well because people do not go to be taxed, the tax-gatherer rather coming to them, as because ἀπογράφεσθαι may have the middle signification, 'to register or enrol themselves.' Alford translates in the sense of 'being enrolled,' that is, passively, both here and in *v.* 1, and in the middle signification in *v.* 5. Jerome, with more exactness, translates by *describor* and *descriptio* in verses 1 and 2, and by *profiteor* in verses 3 and 5. The fact seems to have been that the general enrolment which first (πρώτη) completely carried out the intention of the decree, took place eight or nine years after the movement consequent upon its promulgation, and that St Luke, to prevent misapprehension, has given intimation of this circumstance in *v.* 2.

More than one learned commentator considers that in Gal. vi. 11 St Paul is referring to large and "unsightly" letters, which it is supposed he was compelled to write in consequence of defective vision. But St Paul does not himself advert here to any such defect, and therefore, whether the fact were so or not, it is unjustifiable to make the sense of the passage depend upon it. Probably the supposed circumstance has no other foundation than the disposition of some modern biblical critics to seize upon whatever appears to be evidence of weakness on the part of St Paul, whether bodily or intellectual. But the expression 'with my own hand' should have protected him from the imputation of making this trivial statement, inasmuch as it would be superfluous for any one who is confessing that he writes in "unsightly characters" to say that he writes them with his own hand. The fact is St Paul usually wrote by an amanuensis (see Rom. xvi. 22), and, accordingly, in the most natural way possible, at the end of a long letter written with his own hand, he states this circumstance to the Galatians in attestation of his regard for them and solicitude concerning their spiritual interests. The objection that St Paul does not use γράμματα for an epistle, is completely met by saying that this word is so used by St Luke (Acts xxviii. 21); for surely St Paul might employ the same vocabulary that his fellow-labourer did.

Another commentator remarks on Rom. vi. 7, viz. 'he that is dead is justified from sin,' that "a dead man has done with sin; he cannot commit it." This comment leaves out of account the most significant word (δεδικαίωται) of the sentence, and makes St Paul assert a truism;

which is altogether inconsistent with the general character of his writing. Want of appreciation of the whole tenor of the Epistle can alone account for such a remark. In the Note to this passage I have endeavoured to point out its meaning, and the great importance of the doctrine it contains.

On consulting, after this Translation was printed, some of the early Editions of the English Bible, I found, somewhat to my surprise, that several of the translations which I considered to be not unimportant improvements upon the Authorized Version, and it had cost me much labor and thought to decide upon, were already in existence, although not introduced into the Edition of 1611. Thus in the Edition of 1566 (the Great Bible), the apodosis of the sentence in Rom. v. 12 begins with 'even so,' and the verse ends with 'all we have sinned.' The insertion of 'we' here is very noteworthy, as giving to the clause a sense almost identical with the translation 'all sin' which I have adopted. In the Edition of 1572 the 'we' is omitted. All the Editions, including even that of 1611, have a full stop at the end of the verse. The colon, and the long parenthesis, must have been introduced into the Authorized Version by a subsequent recension. In the Geneva Bible of 1578 the apodosis begins with 'and so,' although in the Editions of 1585 and 1595 (Parker's Bible) 'even so' is retained. The example set in the Geneva Edition was followed in that of 1611.

Again, with respect to Rom. ix. 15, the translations in the early Editions are very various. In those of 1585 and 1595, printed by C. Barker and his deputies, the translation and the punctuation are thus given: 'I will shew mercy, to whomsoever I shew mercy: and I will have compassion, on whomsoever I have compassion.' This is equivalent to what is proposed in the present translation. In the other Editions the rendering differs more or less from this, and in particular the Geneva Edition of 1578 has, 'I will have mercy on him, to whom I will have mercy, and will have compassion on him, on whom I will have compassion.' This mistranslation probably gave rise to that in the A. V.

In the Edition of 1578, the conclusion of Rom. iv. 1 is rendered 'hath found concerning the flesh,' with a marginal note 'That is, by works.' This is in accordance with what is said in the Note to this passage in p. 33, and with the quotation there adduced from Theodoret. The A. V. has not followed this rendering.

Some explanation must now be given as to what has been aimed at in the general execution and the style of this Translation. I have uniformly endeavoured to express in the idiomatic English of the present day just what the original does, neither more nor less, and, as far as possible, with the same degree of brevity. If now and then recourse has been had to some measure of circumlocution, it was because I could not otherwise effect an *exact* translation. Also in this Translation *the order of the words* in the original is followed as closely as possible,—more closely, I think, than is the case either in A. V. or in the R. A. V. It seemed to me that St Paul studied in his diction both distinctness and *rhythm*, and I consequently thought that the translation might possess these qualities in greater degree in proportion as the order of his words and clauses was adhered to. The execution of the present undertaking may give the means of judging how far this expectation has been fulfilled. One often hears the beauty and rhythm of the English Version spoken of, but it does not seem to be generally considered to what extent it owes these qualities to the original.

There is reason also to say that St Paul had regard to *variety* in his diction. For example, in vii. 15—21 the three words πράσσω, ποιῶ, and κατεργάζομαι appear to be used for the sake of variety only, without distinction as to sense. In this instance I have attempted to represent in the translation the variations in the choice of the words in the original: but in ii. 1—3, where πράσσω and ποιῶ have the same meaning, as is evident from the way in which they are used in v. 3, no corresponding verbal distinction is made in the translation.

The rule of rendering by the same word in English a Greek word which occurs more than once in the same sense, has been strictly attended to. This rule, which is obviously correct in principle, has been much violated in A. V., merely, as it seems, for the sake of variety. It may, however, happen that the same Greek word occurs, even in the same passage, in different senses expressible by different words in English: in which case, of course, different English words are to be used. An instance of this kind, as respects the use of the verb κρίνω, may be seen in xiv. 13. (See the Note to this passage.)

In St Paul's writings we sometimes meet with apparent deviations from strict grammatical construction, which, however, convey distinctly the meaning of the writer, and therefore do not really violate the principles of grammar. Under this head may be placed constructions such as those which occur in Chapter v. As these ellipses are themselves significant, no attempt should be made to fill them up. (See the Note to v. 18.) The ellipsis of the substantive verb is a distinct feature of the language both of the Septuagint and the New Testament, and was probably also a characteristic of the language of ordinary intercourse in the Apostle's time. The practice may probably be attributed to a habit of expression more suited to *concrete description* than to *abstract assertion*, the object or event being mentally regarded as if in view, and therefore not requiring its actuality to be formally stated. Owing to the circumstance that our mode of thought, or mode of expressing thought, takes rather an abstract than a concrete form, it is generally, but not always, necessary to supply the substantive verb in translating into English. For these reasons I am of the opinion that there is no need, when a verb substantive is supplied, to indicate by change of type, or otherwise, that it does not occur in the Greek. In fact, throughout the translation I have not given an indication of that kind, because I consider that Scripture, in common with all intelligible writing, contains all the words that are necessary for conveying precisely the sense intended, and that a translation is only concerned with conveying, by whatever means, exactly the same sense. For instance, in ix. 18 ὃν θέλει is translated 'whom He wills to have mercy on,' and again in the same verse, 'whom He wills to harden,' because the Greek construction shews that in the former case the pronoun ὅν must be governed by ἐλεεῖν understood, and in the other by σκληρύνειν understood.

In conformity with the principle of translating the Epistle into current idiomatic English, I have discarded the *archaisms* of the Authorized Version, retaining only in some few instances the termination *th* of the third person singular of the present tense of verbs, for the sake of variety and dignity of expression, as is done in modern English poetry. In that respect I have deviated from the example set by the Five Revisers, who adhere tenaciously to such words and expressions as 'every whit,' 'listeth,' 'we be,' 'the which,' 'wist,' &c. In some instances their rendering is even more archaic than that of A. V. For example, τὸν ἀπὸ Ναζαρέτ (Joh. i. 46), which in A. V. is simply 'of Nazareth,' they translate 'which is from Nazareth.' Again, Rom. vii. 1 is rendered 'Know ye not, brethren, how that the law hath dominion over a man for so long time as he liveth,' A. V. having in place of 'for so long time as' the less archaic expression 'as long as.' I am unable to see what necessity there is for translating ἡ γὰρ ὕπανδρος γυνὴ τῷ ζῶντι ἀνδρὶ δέδεται νόμῳ (Rom. vii. 2), 'for the woman which hath an husband is bound by the law to her husband while he liveth,' inasmuch as the meaning of the Greek admits of being exactly expressed by translating word for word, 'for a married woman is bound by law to a living husband.' Why should not 'however,' which, with respect to the termination 'ever', has its analogues in other languages, be allowed to supplant the obsolete 'howbeit'? There are in our language few terminal distinctions; but custom has now fully separated between 'who' and 'which,' most probably on account of the advantage thereby gained in respect to distinguishing between persons and things. What reason then can there be for continuing the use of 'which' with reference to persons, in opposition to both the written and the spoken idiom of the day? In the Preface to the Revision of the Gospel of St John (p. viii.) the authors make this statement: "Keeping before us the earlier English versions, from Wickliffe downwards, we have constantly rejected words which presented themselves as the most exact equivalents of the Greek, because they wanted the Biblical garb and sound which we were anxious to preserve." Is it possible that there can exist any valid reason for not translating a Greek word into its exact equivalent? By adopting a principle the very reverse of that above stated the revisers of 1611 produced a work which is readable at the present time; and the example they set ought not to be departed from by those who profess to admire the result of their labors.

It would seem to be a very natural and desirable part of an undertaking set on foot for revising the Authorized Version of the Scriptures to change its idiom into that of the best current English. But strange to say, this axiom, as it might be called, meets at the present time with no favour. In the interval that has elapsed since the last Revision, the English language has acquired force and precision, which writers in magazines and newspapers have not been slow to avail themselves of in giving expression to their views on matters of immediate interest. Why should the more perfect form of the language be exclusively devoted to material concerns, when it may receive as appropriate an application in speaking of interests far greater, and not more remote? An antique idiom tends very much to qualify the estimation formed of the matter it communicates, and a reader or hearer does not readily regard as of vital importance what is conveyed to him in terms unlike those in which he is accustomed to express himself in the actual exigencies of life. A change of the Authorized Version into an idiom more closely resembling that generally spoken, might have the effect of strengthening in the minds of the people the impression of the reality of the truths it contains, and causing it to be read with more of the personal interest which the word of God demands.

Besides, the language of the New Testament, although qualified by the peculiar character of the subjects treated of, must have been the general medium of communication between all parts of the Roman Empire, such as the French language is in Europe at the present time; for otherwise St Paul and St Peter could not have written intelligible Epistles to widely "scattered" churches. Hence it seems to follow, because the circumstances of our time are in various respects analogous to those of the Roman Empire at the epoch of its greatest developement, that an agreement might also exist between the usages of language now prevailing and those of the phase of the Greek language in common use at that epoch*. From having made the trial I feel persuaded that the current English of this nineteenth century falls in more naturally with the genius of the Greek of the New Testament than the English of the sixteenth or seventeenth century. For this reason also I think that the feeling of strangeness incident to passing from one style to the other would quickly disappear.

I propose to conclude this Introduction with a statement of the grounds on which I say in the Preface that this translation is on a special account entitled to receive consideration. In the doctrinal part of the Epistle to the Romans St Paul uses the word "law" in a manner which ought long since to have attracted more attention than it appears to have had. He speaks of "the law of faith" (iii. 27), " the law of sin" in our members (vii. 23), "the law of the spirit of life" and "the law of sin and death" (viii. 2). Now it is a legitimate means, if not the *only* means, of understanding this application of the word "law," to compare it with the use we have been led to make of the same word in the pursuit of *natural science*. In the two uses *law* has precisely the same meaning, only in one case it has reference to what is external and visible, and in the other to what is inward and spiritual. As there are laws of external nature, so are there laws of spirit; and as science has revealed to us that external nature has been evolved and elaborated in accordance with laws, I have ventured to speak of *laws of the spiritual creation*, regarding these terms as embracing in their application all the means by which the spirits of men are formed for an immortal existence. (See the Notes on v. 18 and 19, and on vi. 7.) This view of the analogy between the laws of God's natural kingdom and the laws of His spiritual kingdom throws great light on the doctrine and the gospel preached by St Paul, and appears to be necessary for understanding

---

* That the Greek of the New Testament was not peculiar to it, but belonged to the era, might, I think, be gathered from the character of the ecclesiastical writings in the first and second centuries, and, in particular, from the style of the early apocryphal writings.

INTRODUCTION.   xxxiii

his method of arguing on certain doctrinal questions, as well as for accounting philologically for some peculiarities in the character of his writing. These points may be further illustrated as follows.

The philosophy of nature consists of two distinct parts. In one, which is experimental, we seek to discover, by observation and experiment, *laws* of nature; in the other, which is theoretical, we endeavour either to give *reasons* for the laws by the aid of calculation, or to ascertain their final causes. In an analogous manner the philosophy of the spiritual creation is concerned both with the laws according to which the divine economy is ordered, and also with the final causes of the existence and operation of the laws. Thus St Paul in the early portion of the Epistle to the Romans treats partly of the laws which determine the prevalence and effect of sin, and of the law of the relation of faith to righteousness, and partly of the final causes of these laws, ending at v. 11 with the doctrine of the final cause of the death of the Son of God. Then beginning (at *v.* 12) with διὰ τοῦτο, 'therefore,' he deduces from that doctrine the reasons for the existence of the laws of sin and death, and of righteousness and life, and the eventual righteousness of 'all men,' as resulting, through the grace of Christ, from their operation. Where in the statement of the laws he employs elliptical language (as especially in *v.* 18), it is evident that this is done because the exhibition of the laws is his main object.

Now I think it may be asserted that the recognition of this analogy, in respect to law, between natural science and the spiritual science of Scripture, not only assists much towards comprehending the latter, but may, perhaps, even be said to be in our day *necessary* for that purpose. I expect, however, here to be met by the objection that after so many ages since the promulgation of Christianity nothing new as regards doctrine is likely to be discovered. It is true that no *new doctrine* can be discovered, because the whole doctrine concerning Jesus Christ was fully known and taught in the age of the apostles. But those who urge the above objection are prone to overlook the fact that the knowledge of the gospel, as taught in the apostolic times, was not *retained*. Very shortly after the decease of the first teachers there was a great falling off in that respect, and the eclipse of faith and knowledge which then commenced has continued with little variation up to the present day. What, therefore, we have reason to seek for and to pray for is not the discovery of new doctrine, but a revival of the knowledge of the old. Now it is to be considered that in the dispensation of such favors "the Ruler of the ages" (1 Tim.

i. 17) always operates by *means*. Thus the world existed many centuries before the Son of God was revealed in it, and this great event did not take place till the revolutions of kingdoms and empires had culminated in the establishment of the empire of Rome, and the way had been prepared, by the diffusion of a common language and facility of intercourse between the different provinces of the empire, for spreading the knowledge of the gospel over the whole of the civilized world. Similarly the providence of God may have ordered that after a long course of years the way should be prepared for a return to the true knowledge of the Gospel, such as existed in the first ages of Christianity. For if this knowledge depends on rightly understanding the teaching of St Paul respecting the laws of the spiritual creation, and if he speaks of law in precisely the sense in which we have learnt to regard it in consequence of modern advances in natural science, it is certain that during many centuries in the interval between the promulgation of Christianity and the present day such teaching was not understood*. We in these days ought to consider ourselves greatly favoured if we have been furnished by God's providence with better means of understanding it. It was the contemplation of a similar developement of the divine economy that led St Paul to exclaim, "Oh the depth of the riches of the wisdom and knowledge of God, how unsearchable are His judgments, and untraceable His ways!" But however inscrutable may be the origination of His plans, they are accomplished, as I said before, by intelligible means. A more complete understanding of St Paul's Epistle to the Romans, acquired by the intervention of appropriate indications from physical as well as philological science, might be the means of revealing to us, as it were,

---

* At the time of the Reformation great efforts were made both by Roman Catholics and Protestants, and with equal sincerity, to effect a reformation of *doctrine*, the labors of the former resulting in the Decrees of the Council of Trent, and those of English Protestants in the thirty-nine Articles of the Church of England. One of the facts that convince me that God granted to the English Reformers a greater amount of knowledge than to their contemporaries is their adoption in Art. x. of the expression "*after* the fall of Adam." This manner of assertion conforms to the principle of distinguishing between the statement of a *law* and assigning a *reason*, and as such is a near approach to the views I have been endeavouring to explain. Yet it is now generally taught and believed that "the condition of mankind after the fall" was *contingent* on Adam's sin, which, as I can attest, is called in printed sermons, and by persons in conversation an "unfortunate occurrence." Few, however, seem to be aware how incongruous such language as this is both with the Articles of our Church and the teaching of St Paul. The whole body of Dissenters and Presbyterians appear to have made no progress in religious knowledge in this respect.

a new gospel, which, however, would not be "another" gospel, but a renewed understanding of that which was originally preached.

Although in the above discussion I have referred exclusively to the writings of St Paul, the distinction that exists between the revelations of Scripture concerning the *laws* of God's spiritual kingdom, and those concerning the *purposes* to be accomplished by them, pervades the whole of the Scriptures, and is especially discernible in the discourses and parables of our Lord. But respecting these it would be here out of place to enter upon a discussion.

If then it may be admitted, for the reasons now given, that the recognition of "the reign of law" in the spiritual world as well as in its necessary antecedent, the natural world, and of an analogy between the operations of the two kinds of law, serves to elucidate the doctrine taught by St Paul, it may be further said that such a view will contribute towards improving the *translation* of the Epistle. This assertion may be made on the principle that interpretation and translation are so related, that any accession to the former helps to improve the latter. As an illustration of this dictum I may mention that having had opportunities of seeing translations of scientific memoirs into English, made by persons abundantly qualified as linguists for the undertaking, but wholly unacquainted with the subjects treated of in the originals, I have detected many errors which a competent acquaintance with the subject would have enabled the translator to avoid.

So far then as the recognition of the above-mentioned analogy between the operation of the laws of the natural world and that of the laws of the spiritual world, together with the devotion of much thought to enquiries by the aid of mathematics into the laws of nature, may have been the means of giving me an insight into the doctrine of St Paul and the mode of his teaching, the translation I here produce, which is the fruit of long and anxious labour, may claim in a special manner to receive attention from Biblical students.

I shall only observe farther that in the explanations contained in the Notes it will be found that I have followed out to its *logical* consequences the theory of a spiritual creation governed by determinate laws, in so far as such theory rests upon teaching conveyed by the words of St Paul. The conclusion to which it has conducted respecting the final effect of the operation of the laws, will probably be thought by many to be contradictory to what is declared in other parts of Scripture. No doubt there is here a difficulty, although there may be no real contradiction, and the difficulty may be one which will admit of solution if God should grant in these days a still larger measure of knowledge of His truth. In the mean while something may have been done towards overcoming the difficulty by logical deduction, apart from all other considerations, from the inspired words of an Apostle, and by directing attention to a distinction to be made between the revelations of Scripture which speak of the fixed and unalterable laws of the spiritual creation, and those which declare how by means of communicated knowledge of such laws, and their operation, the eternal purposes of the Omnipotent Creator towards His creation are accomplished.

It may be proper to state here that when the pronouns He, His, Him, occur in the Translation with a capital letter they refer exclusively to God the Father, the distinction being made because it is always either expressed or implied in the original, and often facilitates the understanding of a passage. For this reason also 'Whom' has a capital letter at the end of the Epistle in p. 23.

THE EPISTLE OF THE APOSTLE PAUL

TO

THE ROMANS.

I. ¹PAUL, a called servant of Jesus Christ, an apostle set apart unto the gospel of God, ²which He before promised by His prophets in the holy scriptures, ³concerning His Son, who was made of the seed of David according to flesh, ⁴who was ordained Son of God in power, according to the Spirit of holiness, by reason of the resurrection of the dead, Jesus Christ our Lord; ⁵through whom we received grace and apostleship, unto the obedience of faith among all nations, for the sake of His name; ⁶among whom are ye also, Jesus Christ's called; ⁷to all in Rome who are beloved of God, saints called,—Grace to you and peace from God our Father and the Lord Jesus Christ.

⁸I first thank my God through Jesus Christ concerning you all, that your faith is published throughout the world. ⁹For God is my witness, whom I serve in my spirit in the gospel of His Son, how unceasingly I make mention of you, always in my prayers ¹⁰requesting that by some means I might at length succeed by the will of God in coming to you. ¹¹For I long to see you, that I may impart to you some spiritual gift, to the end that ye may be established: ¹²and this is to be at the same time comforted in you by mutual faith, both yours and mine. ¹³Moreover I would not have you ignorant, brethren, that many times I purposed to come to you—and was hindered hitherto—that I might have some fruit in you also, as well as in the rest of the Gentiles. ¹⁴I am debtor both to Greeks and to Barbarians; both to the wise and the foolish. ¹⁵Hence the readi-

ness that is in me to preach the gospel to you also who are in Rome.

¹⁶ For I am not ashamed of the gospel; for it is the power of God unto salvation to every one that believes, both to the Jew first and to the Greek. ¹⁷ For the righteousness of God is therein revealed from faith unto faith; as it is written, He that is righteous from faith shall live. ¹⁸ For the wrath of God is revealed from heaven against all ungodliness and unrighteousness of men who hold the truth in unrighteousness. ¹⁹ Because that which is known of God is manifest in them; for God has manifested it to them. ²⁰ For the things of Him invisible from the creation of the world, being understood by the things that are made, are clearly seen, both His eternal power and godhead; so that they are without excuse, ²¹ because, knowing God, they glorified Him not as God, nor gave Him thanks; but became empty in their reasonings, and their heart devoid of understanding was darkened. ²² Claiming to be wise, they became fools; ²³ and changed the glory of the incorruptible God into the likeness by an image of corruptible man, and of birds, and four-footed beasts, and creeping things,—²⁴ on account of which God delivered them in the desires of their hearts to uncleanness, to dishonour their bodies among themselves;— ²⁵ who changed the truth of God into a lie, and worshipped and served the creature rather than the Creator, who is blessed for ever. Amen.

²⁶ Therefore God gave them up to shameful affections; for as well their females changed the natural use into that which is against nature, ²⁷ as in like manner the males also, leaving the natural use of the female, burned in their lust one towards another, males with males practising that which is unseemly, and receiving in themselves the recompense of their error which was meet. ²⁸ And as they did not approve having God in their knowledge, God gave them over to a reprobate mind, to do things unfit to be done; ²⁹ being filled with all unrighteousness, wickedness, covetousness, maliciousness; full of envy, murder, strife, deceit, malignity; whisperers, ³⁰ slanderers, haters of God, insolent, proud, boasters, inventors of evil things, disobedient to parents, ³¹ without understanding, covenant breakers, without

natural affection, unmerciful: ³²who knowing the just sentence of God, that they who do such things are worthy of death, not only do the same, but also are consentient with those that do them.

II. ¹Wherefore thou art without excuse, O man, whoever thou art that judgest: for wherein thou judgest another thou condemnest thyself; for thou that judgest doest the same things. ²Now we know that the judgment of God is according to truth against them who do such things: ³but thou thinkest this, O man, that judgest them who do such things and doest the same, that thou wilt escape the judgment of God; ⁴or, thou despisest the riches of his goodness, and forbearance, and long-suffering, not knowing that the goodness of God leads thee to repentance; ⁵and, according to thy hardness and impenitent heart, treasurest up for thyself wrath in the day of wrath and revelation of the righteous judgment of God; ⁶who will render to every man according to his works: ⁷to them who, under patience in well-doing, seek for glory, and honour, and incorruption, eternal life; ⁸but to them that are contentious, and obey not the truth, but obey unrighteousness, will be indignation and wrath; ⁹tribulation and distress upon every soul of man that works evil, both of the Jew first, and of the Greek; ¹⁰but glory, and honour, and peace, to every man that works good, both to the Jew first, and to the Greek. ¹¹For there is no respect of persons with God. ¹²For as many as without law have sinned, without law also will perish; and as many as have sinned in law, through law will be judged. ¹³For not the hearers of the law are just before God, but the doers of the law will be justified. ¹⁴For when Gentiles who have not the law do by nature the things of the law, these, not having the law, are law to themselves: ¹⁵who shew the work of the law written in their hearts, their conscience witnessing with them, and their thoughts one with another accusing, or also excusing, ¹⁶in the day when God will judge the secrets of men, according to my gospel, by Jesus Christ.

¹⁷But if thou art called a Jew, and restest on the law, and makest thy boast in God, ¹⁸and knowest His will, and approvest things that are excellent, being instructed out of the law; ¹⁹and art confident that thou thyself art a guide of the blind, a light of them who are in darkness, ²⁰an instructor of the foolish, a

teacher of babes, having the form of knowledge and truth in the law: ²¹thou, then, who teachest another teachest not thyself; thou that preachest, steal not, stealest; ²²thou that sayest, commit not adultery, committest adultery; thou that abhorrest idols, committest sacrilege; ²³thou that boastest in the law, through transgression of the law dishonourest God. ²⁴For the name of God because of you is blasphemed among the Gentiles, as it is written. ²⁵For circumcision is profitable if thou do the law; but if thou be a transgressor of the law thy circumcision has become uncircumcision. ²⁶If then he that is uncircumcised keep the ordinances of the law, shall not his uncircumcision be reckoned for circumcision? ²⁷And shall not the uncircumcision which is from nature, by fulfilling the law, judge thee who through the letter and circumcision art a transgressor of the law? ²⁸For he is not a Jew who is one outwardly; neither is circumcision that which is outward in the flesh; ²⁹but he is a Jew who is one inwardly, and circumcision is of the heart, in spirit, not in letter; whose praise is not from men but from God.

III. ¹What then the advantage of the Jew, or what the profit of circumcision? ²Much every way: chiefly, indeed, because they were entrusted with the oracles of God.

³What now? if some men have not believed, shall their unbelief make God's faithfulness of no effect? ⁴May it not be! let God be true, and every man a liar,—as it is written—That thou mightest be justified in thy sayings, and mightest overcome when thou art judged. ⁵But if our unrighteousness constitutes the righteousness of God, what shall we say? Is God who inflicts wrath unrighteous? (I speak as a man.) ⁶May it not be! for then how shall God judge the world? ⁷Now if the truth of God abounded in my lie unto his glory, why yet am even I judged as a sinner? ⁸And why is it not (as we are blasphemed, and as some affirm that we say), that we should do the evil things that the good things of which the judgment is just may come?

⁹What then? do we excel? In no manner: for we before proved that both Jews and Greeks are all under sin; ¹⁰as it is written, there is not a just man, not even one; ¹¹there is no one that understands, there is no one that seeks after God; ¹²all have gone

out of the way, they are together become unprofitable; there is no one that doeth good, there is not so much as one. ¹³Their throat is an open sepulchre; with their tongues they are wont to deceive; the poison of asps is under their lips; ¹⁴whose mouth is full of cursing and bitterness; ¹⁵their feet are swift to shed blood; ¹⁶destruction and misery are in their ways; ¹⁷and the way of peace they have not known: ¹⁸there is no fear of God before their eyes. ¹⁹Now we know that what the law says it speaks to them that are in the law, that every mouth may be stopped, and all the world become guilty before God. ²⁰Because from works of law shall no flesh be justified in His sight: for through law is the knowledge of sin.

²¹ But now apart from law the righteousness of God has been manifested, being witnessed by the law and the prophets; ²²but the righteousness of God through faith of Jesus Christ unto all and upon all them that believe; for there is no difference: ²³for all have sinned and are destitute of the glory of God; ²⁴being justified freely by His grace through the redemption which is in Christ Jesus, ²⁵whom God set forth as a propitiation, through faith, in his blood, for shewing forth His righteousness, on account of the remission of antecedent sins, in the forbearance of God; ²⁶for shewing forth His righteousness in the present time, that He may be just and make just him who is of the faith of Jesus. ²⁷Where then is boasting? It is excluded. By what kind of law? One of works? No, but by a law of faith. ²⁸For we reckon that a man is justified by faith, apart from works of the law. ²⁹Is God the God of the Jews only? not also of the Gentiles? Yes, of the Gentiles also; ³⁰since God is one, who will justify the circumcision from faith, and the uncircumcision through faith. ³¹Do we then make void the law through faith? May it not be! Rather; we establish the law.

IV. ¹What then shall we say that Abraham our father has obtained according to flesh? ²For as Abraham was justified from works he has something to boast of. But not as regards God. ³For what saith Scripture? Abraham believed God, and it was reckoned to him unto righteousness. ⁴Now to him who works the pay is not reckoned as a favour but as a debt. ⁵But to him who works not, but believes on Him who justifies the ungodly, his faith is reckoned unto righteousness. [6]As David also pronounces the man to be blessed to whom God reckons righteousness apart from works :—[7] Blessed are they whose iniquities are forgiven and whose sins are covered ; [8]blessed is the man to whom the Lord will not reckon sin. [9]Is then this blessing pronounced upon the circumcision, or also upon the uncircumcision ? For we say that faith was reckoned to Abraham unto righteousness. [10]How then was it reckoned to him ? when he was in circumcision, or in uncircumcision ? Not in circumcision, but in uncircumcision ; [11]and he received the sign of circumcision, a seal of the righteousness from the faith which he had in uncircumcision, in order that he might be father of all who believe through uncircumcision to the end that to them also righteousness might be reckoned, [12]and father of circumcision to those not of the circumcision only, but also to those who walk in the steps of the faith in uncircumcision of our father Abraham. [13]For the promise to Abraham, or to his seed, was not that through law he should be heir of the world, but through the righteousness of faith. [14]For if they who are of the law be heirs, faith has been made void and the promise made of no effect. [15]For the law works wrath : for where there is not law, neither is there transgression. [16]On this account it is of faith, that it may be according to grace; to the end that the promise may be sure to all the seed ; not only to that which is of the law, but also to that which is of the faith of Abraham ; who is the father of us all—[17]as it is written, a father of many nations have I made thee—before that God whom he believed, who makes the dead alive, and calls things that are not as if they were. [18]Who against hope in hope believed, that he might become father of many nations, according to that which was spoken, So shall thy seed be; [19]and not being weak in faith, considered his own body now become dead, he being about a hundred years old, and the deadness of Sarah's womb, [20]yet did not waver at the promise of God through unbelief, but was confirmed by faith, giving glory to God [21]and being fully persuaded that what He has promised He is able also to perform. [22]Wherefore also it was reckoned to him unto righteousness. [23]Now it was not written for the sake of him only that it was reckoned to him, ²⁴but for the sake of us also, to whom it will be reckoned, we being believers on Him who raised Jesus our Lord from the dead ; ²⁵who was delivered up on account of our offences, and was raised on account of our justification.

V. ¹Being, then, justified from faith, we have peace with God through our Lord Jesus Christ, (²through whom also we have had access by faith into this grace in which we stand), and we rejoice in hope of the glory of God. ³And not only so, but we also rejoice in tribulations, knowing that tribulation works patience, ⁴and patience experience, and experience hope ; ⁵and hope makes not ashamed because the love of God has been poured forth in our hearts by the Holy Spirit which was given to us. ⁶For while we were yet without strength, in due season Christ died for the ungodly. ⁷For scarcely for a righteous man will any one die : for in behalf of that which is good perhaps some one even dares to die. ⁸But God makes manifest the love of Himself towards us, because while we were yet sinners Christ died for us. ⁹Much rather then, being now justified in his blood, shall we be saved through him from the wrath. ¹⁰For if, being enemies, we were reconciled to God through the death of His Son, much rather, being reconciled, shall we be saved in his life; ¹¹and not only so, but as also rejoicing in God through our Lord Jesus Christ, through whom we have now received the reconciliation.

¹²Therefore, as through one man sin entered into the world, and through sin, death, also in this manner death passed unto all men, for that all sin. ¹³For until the law sin was in the world, although sin is not taken into account when there is not law. ¹⁴But death reigned from Adam to Moses even over them who did not sin after the manner of the transgression of Adam, who is a type of that which was to be. ¹⁵But not as the offence, so also the favour. For if by the offence of the one the many died, much more did the grace of God, and the gift in grace, the grace of the one man Jesus Christ, abound to the many. ¹⁶And not as through one sin the bestowal of the favour. For judgment is from one offence to condemnation; but the favour from many offences unto justification. ¹⁷For if in one offence death reigned through the one man, much more shall they who

receive the abundance of grace and of the gift of righteousness reign in life through the one Jesus Christ. ¹⁸Therefore, as by one offence, unto all men, to condemnation; so also through one justification, unto all men, to righteousness of life. ¹⁹For as through the disobedience of the one man the many were made sinners, so also through the obedience of the One shall the many be made righteous. ²⁰The law meanwhile came in that the offence might increase; but where sin increased, grace did still more abound; ²¹that as sin reigned in death, so also grace might reign through righteousness unto eternal life through Jesus Christ our Lord.

VI. ¹What then shall we say? Should we continue in sin that grace may abound? ²May it not be! How shall we who die to sin live any longer therein? ³Know ye not that as many of us as were baptized into Jesus Christ were baptized into his death? ⁴We were, therefore, buried with him through baptism into death, that as Christ was raised up after death through the glory of the Father, so also we should walk in newness of life. ⁵For as we have become akin to him by likeness as to his death, moreover we shall be by likeness as to resurrection: ⁶knowing this, that our old man was crucified with him, that the sinful body might be destroyed, that we should no longer serve sin. ⁷For he that is dead has been justified from sin. ⁸Now if we die with Christ, we believe that we shall also live with him: ⁹knowing that Christ, being raised up after death, dies no more; death has no more dominion over him. ¹⁰For that which dies, dies to sin at once; but that which lives, lives to God. ¹¹Thus also reckon ye yourselves dead indeed to sin, but living to God in Christ Jesus.

¹²Let not sin then reign in your mortal body unto obeying the body's lusts; ¹³neither yield your members to sin as instruments of unrighteousness; but yield yourselves to God, as if living after death, and your members to God, as instruments of righteousness. ¹⁴For sin will not have dominion over you; for ye are not under law but under grace.

¹⁵What then? Should we sin because we are not under law but under grace? May it not be! ¹⁶Know ye not that so far as ye yield yourselves servants unto obedience, ye are servants to

that which ye obey, whether servants sinful unto death, or obedient unto righteousness. [17] But thanks be to God that ye are no longer servants of sin, but obeyed from the heart the form of doctrine into which ye were delivered. [18] Being made free from sin ye served righteousness. [19] (I speak after the manner of men because of the infirmity of your flesh). For as ye yielded your members servants to uncleanness, and to iniquity unto iniquity, so now yield your members servants to righteousness unto holiness. [20] For when ye were servants of sin, ye were free from service to righteousness. [21] What fruit, then, had ye at that time in those things of which ye are now ashamed? For the end of those things is death. [22] But now having been freed from sin, and become servants to God, ye have your fruit unto holiness, and the end eternal life. [23] For the wages of sin is death; but the gift of God is eternal life in Christ Jesus our Lord.

VII. [1] Know ye not, brethren, (for I speak to them who know the law) that the law has dominion over a man as long as he lives. [2] For a married woman is bound by law to a living husband; but if the husband die, she is released from the law of the husband. [3] Therefore, the husband being alive, she will be called an adulteress if she be joined to another man: but if the husband be dead, she is free from the law, so as not to be an adulteress by being joined to another man. [4] So that, my brethren, ye also were put to death to the law through the body of Christ, to the intent that ye should be joined to another, to him who was raised up after death, in order that we might bring forth fruit to God. [5] For when we were in the flesh, the passions of sins,—passions that are through the law,—wrought in our members to bring forth fruit to death. [6] But now we are released from the law, being dead,—the law in which we were held,—so that we serve in the newness of spirit, not in the oldness of letter.

[7] What then shall we say? Is the law sin? May it not be! Rather, I had not known sin except through the law; for I had not known coveting unless the law had said, Thou shalt not covet. [8] Sin, taking occasion, through the commandment wrought in me all manner of coveting. For apart from law sin is dead.

⁹I was living at one time apart from law; but the commandment coming, sin rose into life, ¹⁰but I died; and the commandment that was unto life, this was found by me to be unto death. ¹¹For sin, taking occasion, through the commandment deceived me, and through it slew me. ¹²So that the law is holy, and the commandment holy, and just, and good.

¹³Did, then, that which is good become death to me? May it not be! Rather, sin became death to me, that sin might appear working death to me through that which is good, in order that sin might become above measure sinful through the commandment. ¹⁴For we know that the law is spiritual; but I am carnal, sold under sin. ¹⁵For what I perform I know not: for not what I would, this I practise; but what I hate, this I do. ¹⁶Now if what I would not, this I do, I assent to the law, that it is good: ¹⁷but thus no longer I perform it, but the sin that dwells in me. ¹⁸For I know that in me, that is, in my flesh, no good thing dwells. For willingness is present with me, but not the performance of what is good. ¹⁹For the good that I would I do not; but the evil that I would not, this I do. ²⁰But if what myself would not, this I do, no longer I perform it, but the sin that dwells in me. ²¹I find, therefore, the law, to me who am willing to do good, that to me evil is present. ²²For I delight in the law of God according to the inner man: ²³but I see another law in my members warring against the law of my mind, and bringing me into captivity to the law of sin which is in my members. ²⁴Wretched man that I am! who shall deliver me from this deathful body? ²⁵I am thankful to God through Jesus Christ our Lord. Therefore I myself with the mind serve the law of God, but with the flesh the law of sin.

VIII. ¹There is, therefore, now no condemnation to them who are in Christ Jesus. ²For the law of the spirit of life in Christ Jesus freed thee from the law of sin and death. ³For what the law could not do, in that it was weak through the flesh, God sending His own Son in the likeness of sinful flesh, and with reference to sin, condemned sin in the flesh, ⁴that the righteousness of the law might be fulfilled in us who walk not according to flesh but according to spirit. ⁵For they who are according to flesh mind the things of the flesh; but they who are according to spirit the things of the spirit. ⁶For the fleshly mind is death, but the spiritual mind life and peace. ⁷Because the fleshly mind is enmity against God; for it is not subject to the law of God; for neither can it be. ⁸They who are in the flesh cannot please God. ⁹But ye are not in flesh but in spirit, if the Spirit of God dwells in you. But if any one has not the Spirit of Christ, this man is not his. ¹⁰Now if Christ be in you, the body indeed is dead because of sin, but the spirit is life because of righteousness. ¹¹And if the Spirit of Him who raised up Jesus after death dwells in you, He who raised up Christ after death will make alive also your mortal bodies because of His Spirit dwelling in you.

¹²Therefore, brethren, debtors we are not to the flesh, in respect to living according to flesh: ¹³for if ye live according to flesh, ye are ready to die; but if by the Spirit ye put to death the deeds of the body, ye will live. ¹⁴For as many as are led by the Spirit of God, these are sons of God. ¹⁵For ye did not receive the spirit of service again unto fear, but ye received the spirit of adoption, in which we cry, Abba, Father. ¹⁶The Spirit itself bears witness with our spirit that we are children of God. ¹⁷And if children, also heirs; heirs of God, and joint-heirs with Christ; since we suffer with him, that we may also be glorified with him.

¹⁸For I reckon that the sufferings of the present time are of no account in comparison with the glory that is to be revealed in us. ¹⁹For the earnest expectation of the creation waits for the revelation of the sons of God. ²⁰For the creation became subject to vanity, not of its own accord, but on account of Him who made it subject in anticipation ²¹that even the creation itself will be freed from the bondage of corruption into the liberty of the glory of the children of God. ²²For we know that the whole creation groans together, and travails in pain together, until now. ²³Not only so, but also ourselves who have the first-fruits of the Spirit, even we ourselves groan within ourselves waiting for adoption, the redemption of our body. ²⁴For we are saved by hope. But a hope that is seen is not a hope; for that which any one sees why does he also hope for? ²⁵But if we hope for what we see not, we wait for it with patience.

²⁶ In the same manner also the Spirit helps our weakness. For what we might pray for as it becomes us we know not: but the Spirit itself intercedes in our behalf with groanings that cannot be spoken; ²⁷ and He who searches hearts, knows what is the mind of the Spirit, because He intercedes for the saints according to God.

²⁸ And we know that to them who love God all things work together for good, to them who are the called according to purpose. ²⁹ Because whom He foreknew, them He also foreordained to be together in the form of the image of His Son, that he might be the firstborn among many brethren; ³⁰ and whom He foreordained, them He also called; and whom He called, them He also justified; and whom He justified, them He also glorified.

³¹ What then shall we say, these things being so? If God is for us, who is against us? ³² He that spared not His own Son, but delivered him up for us all, how shall He not also with him freely give us all things? ³³ Who shall bring accusation against God's elect? Shall God who justifies? ³⁴ Who is he that condemns? Christ Jesus who died? rather, who has risen? who is also at the right hand of God? who also intercedes for us? ³⁵ Who shall separate us from the love of God? Shall tribulation, or distress, or persecution, or famine, or nakedness, or peril, or sword? ³⁶ (As it is written: For thy sake we are killed all day long, we are accounted as sheep for the slaughter.) ³⁷ Nay, in all these things we more than conquer through him who loved us. ³⁸ For I am persuaded that neither death, nor life, nor angels, nor principalities, nor things present, nor things to come, nor powers, ³⁹ nor height, nor depth, nor any other creation, will be able to separate us from the love of God which is in Christ Jesus our Lord.

IX. ¹ I say the truth in Christ, I lie not, my conscience bearing witness with me in the Holy Spirit, ² that I have great sorrow and continual anguish in my heart; ³ for I myself desired to be accursed from Christ in behalf of my brethren, my kinsmen according to the flesh; ⁴ who are Israelites; to whom belong the adoption, and the glory, and the covenants, and the giving of the law, and the service, and the promises; ⁵ whose are the fathers, and from whom, in respect to flesh, is Christ, who is over all God blessed for ever. Amen.

⁶Not so, however, as that the word of God has failed. For they who are of Israel, these are not all Israel, ⁷neither because they are Abraham's seed are they all children: but, In Isaac shall thy seed be called. ⁸That is, the children of the flesh, these are not the children of God, but the children of promise are reckoned for seed. ⁹For the word of promise is this: According to this season I will come, and Sarah shall have a son. ¹⁰And not so only, but also there is Rebecca, conceiving by one, our father Isaac. ¹¹For the children being not yet born, neither having done any thing good or evil, that the purpose of God according to election might remain, not of works, but of one who calls, ¹²it was said to her, The elder shall serve the younger: ¹³as it is written, Jacob I loved, but Esau I hated. ¹⁴What then shall we say? Is there unrighteousness with God? May it not be! ¹⁵For He saith to Moses, I will have mercy, whomsoever I may have mercy upon; and I will have compassion, whomsoever I may have compassion upon. ¹⁶Therefore it is not of one that wills, neither of one that runs, but of God shewing mercy. ¹⁷For the Scripture says to Pharaoh, For this very purpose I raised thee up, that I might shew forth my power in thee, and that my name might be published in all the earth. ¹⁸Therefore whom He wills to have mercy on, He has mercy on, and whom He wills to harden, He hardens. ¹⁹Thou wilt then say to me, Why does He yet find fault? For who resists His will? ²⁰In deed, O man! who art thou that repliest against God? shall the thing formed say to him that formed it, why hast thou made me thus? ²¹Or, has not the potter power over the clay, of the same lump to make one vessel unto honour, and another unto dishonour? ²²Now if God, willing to shew wrath and make known His power endured in much long-suffering vessels of wrath fitted for destruction, ²³it was that He might make known the riches of His glory on vessels of mercy which He before prepared for glory; ²⁴us whom He also called, not only of the Jews, but also of the Gentiles: ²⁵As also He saith in Hosea, I will call them my people who were not my people, and her beloved who was not beloved; ²⁶and it shall be, in the place

where it was said to them, ye are not my people, there shall they be called sons of the living God. [27]But Isaiah cries concerning Israel, If the number of the sons of Israel should be as the sand of the sea, that which remains will be saved. [28]For He is finishing the work, and completing it in righteousness; for a complete work will the Lord perform on the earth. [29]And as Isaiah said before, Unless the Lord of Sabaoth had left us a seed, we should have been as Sodom, and become like as Gomorrah.

[30]What then shall we say? That Gentiles who follow not after righteousness took hold of righteousness, the righteousness which is from faith; [31]but Israel, following after the law of righteousness, did not attain to that law. [32]Wherefore? Because it was not from faith, but as it were from works. They stumbled at the stone of stumbling; [33]as it is written, Behold I lay in Zion a stone of stumbling and rock of offence, and he who believes thereon shall not be ashamed.

X. [1]Brethren, the desire of my heart and prayer to God in their behalf is for their salvation. [2]For I bear witness to them that they have a zeal of God, but not according to knowledge. [3]For not knowing the righteousness of God, and seeking to establish their own righteousness, they have not submitted themselves to the righteousness of God. [4]For Christ is the end of the law unto righteousness to every one that believes. [5]For Moses writes respecting the righteousness which is of the law, The man who doeth them shall live in them. [6]But the righteousness from faith speaks thus: Say not in thine heart, Who shall ascend into heaven? that is, to bring Christ down: [7]or, Who shall descend into the abyss? that is, to bring up Christ from the dead. [8]But what does it say? The word is nigh thee, in thy mouth and in thy heart, that is, the word of faith which we preach: [9]That if thou shalt confess with thy mouth the Lord Jesus, and shalt believe in thy heart, that God raised him up after death, thou wilt be saved. [10]For with the heart man believes unto righteousness, and with the mouth confession is made unto salvation. [11]For the Scripture says, No one who believes on him shall be ashamed. [12]For there is no difference between Jew and Greek; for there is the same Lord of all, who is rich towards all that call upon him. ¹³For whosoever shall call upon the name of the Lord will be saved.

¹⁴How then shall they call on him in whom they have not believed? and how shall they believe in him of whom they have not heard? and how shall they hear without a preacher? ¹⁵and how shall they preach unless they be sent? As it is written, How beautiful the feet of those who preach the gospel of peace, who preach the gospel of good things! ¹⁶But they did not all hearken to the gospel. For Isaiah says, Lord, who has believed our report? ¹⁷(So then faith is from hearing, and hearing through the word of God.) ¹⁸But I say, did they not hear? In truth, their voice went out unto all the earth, and their words to the bounds of the world. ¹⁹But I say, did not Israel know? First of all Moses says, I will provoke you to jealousy with that which is not a nation, and with a foolish nation I will anger you. ²⁰But Isaiah is very bold and says, I was found by them who sought me not, I became manifest to them who enquired not after me. ²¹But as regards Israel he says, All the day I stretched forth my hands towards a disobedient and gainsaying people.

XI. ¹I say then, has God cast off His people? May it not be! for I also am an Israelite, of the seed of Abraham, of the tribe of Benjamin. ²God has not cast off His people whom He foreknew. Know ye not what the Scripture says in Elijah, how he pleads with God against Israel? ³Lord, they have killed thy prophets, they have digged down thy altars, and I only am left, and they seek my life. ⁴But what saith the divine oracle to him? I have left remaining for myself seven thousand men who have not bowed the knee to Baal. ⁵Thus, therefore, even in the present time there is a remnant according to the election of grace. ⁶(But if by grace, no longer of works; otherwise grace is no longer grace). ⁷What then? That which Israel seeks for he has not obtained; but the election has obtained, and the rest were blinded—⁸as it is written, God gave them a spirit of slumber, eyes not to see, and ears not to hear—unto the present day. ⁹And David says, Let their table become a snare, and a trap, and a stumbling-block, and a recompence to them: ¹⁰let their eyes be darkened so that they see not, and bow down their back continually.

¹¹ I say then, did they stumble to the end that they should fall? May it not be! Rather, by their fall is salvation to the Gentiles, to provoke them to jealousy. ¹²Now if the fall of them be the riches of the world, and the diminishing of them the riches of the Gentiles, how much rather their fulness! ¹³(I am speaking to you Gentiles: inasmuch, then, as I am the apostle of the Gentiles, I glorify my office, ¹⁴if by any means I may provoke to jealousy my own flesh and save some of them.) ¹⁵For if the rejection of them be the reconciling of the world, what shall reception into favour be but life after death? ¹⁶And if the firstfruit be holy, such also is the lump; and if the root be holy, such are also the branches. ¹⁷Now if some of the branches were broken off, and thou, being a wild olive, wast grafted in among them, and becamest a partaker of the root and fatness of the olive, ¹⁸boast not against the branches. But if thou boastest against them, thou bearest not the root, but the root bears thee. ¹⁹Thou wilt say then, The branches were broken off that I might be grafted in. ²⁰Well; by reason of unbelief they were broken off, and thou standest by faith: be not high minded, but fear. ²¹For if God spared not the natural branches, neither will he spare thee. ²²Behold, therefore, the goodness and the severity of God: towards them who fell is severity; but towards thee the goodness of God if thou continue in goodness; otherwise thou also wilt be cut off; ²³and they, if they continue not in unbelief, will be grafted in; for God is able to graft them in again. ²⁴For if thou wast cut from an olive wild by nature, and contrary to nature wast grafted into a good olive, much rather will these the natural branches be grafted into their own olive. ²⁵(For I would not that ye should be ignorant, brethren, of this mystery, lest ye be wise in your own conceits, that blindness in part has befallen Israel until the completion of the nations has come in; ²⁶and thus all Israel shall be saved: as it is written, The deliverer will come from Zion, will turn away ungodliness from Jacob, ²⁷and this is to them the covenant from me, when I take away their sins.) ²⁸With regard to the gospel, they are enemies on your account; with regard to the election they are beloved on account of the fathers. ²⁹For the gifts and calling of God are without repentance. ³⁰For as ye formerly did

not believe God, but now have obtained mercy by reason of their unbelief, ³¹so also these have now not believed by reason of your mercy, that they also may obtain mercy. ³²For God has shut up together all in unbelief, that He may have mercy upon all. ³³Oh the depth of the riches both of the wisdom and knowledge of God! How unsearchable are His judgments, and untraceable His ways! ³⁴For who has known the mind of the Lord? or who has been His counsellor? ³⁵or who has first given to Him, and shall be recompensed in return? ³⁶Because from Him, and through Him, and unto Him, are all things: to Him be glory for ever. Amen.

XII. ¹I exhort you, therefore, brethren, through the mercies of God to present your bodies a living sacrifice, holy, acceptable to God,—your reasonable service,—²and not to fashion yourselves according to this world, but to be transformed by the renewing of your mind, that ye may discern what the will of God is, what is good, and acceptable, and perfect. ³For I say, through the grace given to me, to every one that is among you, not to be minded above what he ought to be, but to be minded unto sobermindedness, according as God has dealt to each a measure of faith. ⁴For as in one body we have many members, and the members have not all the same office, ⁵so we being many, are one body in Christ, and severally members one of another,—⁶but having gifts differing according to the grace given to us; whether the gift of prophecy, according to the proportion of faith, ⁷or the gift of ministration, in the ministry,—whether he who teaches, in teaching; ⁸or he who exhorts, in exhortation; he who gives, in simplicity; he who rules, in diligence; he who is merciful, in cheerfulness. ⁹Our love without hypocrisy; haters of that which is evil, cleaving to that which is good; ¹⁰affectionate towards one another in brotherly love; in honour preferring one another; ¹¹in duty not slothful; fervent in spirit; serving the Lord; ¹²rejoicing in hope; patient in tribulation; persevering in prayer; ¹³sharing in the necessities of the saints; given to hospitality. ¹⁴Bless them who persecute you; bless, and curse not. ¹⁵Rejoice with them that rejoice; weep with them that weep; ¹⁶being of the same mind one towards another; not minding high things, but acquiescing in things that are lowly. Be not wise in your own conceits. ¹⁷Repay no man evil for evil. Provide things honest in the sight of all men. ¹⁸If as far as depends on you it be possible, be at peace with all men. ¹⁹Avenge not yourselves, beloved, but give place to anger; for it is written, Vengeance is mine, I will repay, saith the Lord. ²⁰If, therefore, thine enemy hunger, feed him; if he thirst, give him drink. For by doing this thou wilt heap coals of fire on his head. ²¹Be not overcome by evil, but overcome evil in good.

XIII. ¹Let every soul be subject to the higher powers: for there is no power except from God; those that are have been ordained by God. ²So that he who opposes a power resists an ordinance of God; and they who resist will bring on themselves judgment. ³For rulers do not deter from a good work, but from an evil. Thou desirest to be not afraid of the power; do that which is good, and thou wilt have praise from the same: ⁴for it is a servant of God to thee for good. But if thou do that which is evil, be afraid; for it bears not the sword in vain: for it is an avenging servant of God for wrath upon him that doeth evil: ⁵on which account it is necessary to be subject not only because of the wrath, but also for conscience sake; (⁶for on this account ye also pay tribute); for there are ministers of God attending continually to this very thing.

⁷Pay to all their dues: tribute to whom ye owe tribute, custom to whom custom, fear to whom fear, honour to whom honour. ⁸Owe no man anything, except love one towards another; for he who loves another has fulfilled the law. ⁹For this, Thou shalt not commit adultery, Thou shalt not kill, Thou shalt not steal, Thou shalt not bear false witness, Thou shalt not covet, with every other commandment, is summed up in this saying, namely, Thou shalt love thy neighbour as thyself. ¹⁰Love works no ill to a neighbour, therefore love is fulfilment of the law. ¹¹And this, knowing the season, that it is already time for us to awake out of sleep, for now is our salvation nearer than when we believed. ¹²The night is far spent, the day is at hand; let us, therefore, cast off the works of darkness, and let us put on the armour of light. ¹³As if in the day, let us walk becomingly; not in revelling and drunkenness, not in chambering and wantonness, not in strife and envying. ¹⁴But

put ye on the Lord Jesus Christ, and bestow not forethought upon lusts of the flesh.

XIV. ¹Him that is weak in faith receive ye,—not for the sifting of doubts. ²One man believes that he may eat all things; he who is weak eats herbs. ³Let not him that eats, despise him who eats not; and let not him that eats not, judge him who eats: for God has received him. ⁴Who art thou that judgest another's servant? To his own Lord he stands or falls. But he shall stand; for the Lord is able to make him stand. ⁵One man esteems one day above another; another man esteems every day. Let each be fully persuaded in his own mind. ⁶He that regards the day regards it to the Lord; and he that eats, eats to the Lord; for he gives thanks to God: and he that eats not, to the Lord eats not, and gives thanks to God. ⁷For no one of us lives to himself, and no one dies to himself. ⁸For whether we live, we live to the Lord; and whether we die, we die to the Lord: whether, therefore, we live or die, we are the Lord's. ⁹For to this end Christ died and lived, that he might be Lord both of the dead and the living. ¹⁰But thou, why judgest thou thy brother? or thou also, why despisest thou thy brother? For we shall all stand before the judgment-seat of God. ¹¹For it is written, As I live, saith the Lord, every knee shall bow to me, and every tongue shall confess to God. ¹²Therefore every one of us will give account concerning himself to God.

¹³Then let us not judge one another any more; but judge ye of this rather, the not putting a stumbling-block, or an occasion of offence, before a brother. ¹⁴I know and am persuaded in the Lord Jesus that nothing is unclean of itself; only to him who accounts any thing to be unclean, to that man it is unclean. ¹⁵For if because of meat thy brother is grieved, no longer walkest thou according to love. Destroy not by thy meat him for whom Christ died. ¹⁶Let not then your good be evil spoken of. ¹⁷For the kingdom of God is not meat and drink; but righteousness, and peace and joy in the Holy Spirit. ¹⁸For he that in this serves Christ is well-pleasing to God and approved by men. ¹⁹Therefore let us follow after the things that belong to peace, and the things that belong to mutual edi-

fication. ²⁰Do not for the sake of meat undo the work of God. All things indeed are pure; but there is evil to the man who eats with offence. ²¹It is good to abstain from eating flesh, or drinking wine, or from anything wherein thy brother stumbles, or is offended, or is weak. ²²Thou hast faith; have it to thyself before God. Happy is he who judges not himself in that which he approves. ²³But he who doubts, if he should eat, is already condemned, because it is not from faith, and whatever is not from faith is sin.

XV. ¹We that are strong ought to bear the infirmities of the weak, and not to please ourselves. ²Let every one of us please his neighbour in respect to what is good, with a view to edification. ³For Christ also pleased not himself; but, as it is written, The reproaches of them that reproach thee fell on me. ⁴For whatever things were before written, were written for our instruction, that through patience, and through comfort from the Scriptures, we may have hope. ⁵And may the God of patience and of comfort grant you to be of the same mind one toward another, according to Christ Jesus; ⁶that with one accord ye may with one mouth glorify God, the Father of our Lord Jesus Christ. ⁷Wherefore receive ye one another, as Christ also received you, to the glory of God. ⁸For I say that Jesus Christ has become a minister of the circumcision because of God's truth, in order to confirm the promises made to the fathers, ⁹but that the gentiles glorify God because of His mercy: as it is written, For this cause I will give thanks to thee among the gentiles, and will sing to thy name. ¹⁰And again he saith, Rejoice, ye gentiles, with His people: ¹¹and again, Praise the Lord, all ye gentiles, and laud Him all ye peoples. ¹²And again, Isaiah saith, There shall be the root of Jesse and he that arises to rule over the gentiles; in him shall the gentiles hope. ¹³May the God of hope fill you with all joy and peace in believing, that ye may abound in hope in the power of the Holy Spirit.

¹⁴Now I, on my part, am persuaded, my brethren, concerning you, that ye, on your parts, are full of goodness, being filled with all knowledge, able also to admonish one another. ¹⁵I have, however, written to you, brethren, somewhat boldly,

(partly as putting you in mind), on account of the grace given to me by God, [16]that I should be a minister of Jesus Christ for the gentiles, performing a priest's office towards the gospel of God in order that the presenting of the gentiles for an offering may be acceptable, being sanctified in the Holy Spirit. [17]I have, therefore, boasting in Christ Jesus as to the things which pertain to God. [18]For I will not dare to speak of any things other than those which Christ wrought through me, by word and deed, [19]in the power of signs and wonders, in the power of the Spirit of God; so that from Jerusalem, and in a circuit as far as to Illyricum, I have accomplished the preaching of the gospel of Christ, [20]striving by this course to preach the gospel not where Christ was named, lest I should build on another man's foundation: [21]but, as it is written, They to whom no announcement was made concerning him shall see, and they who have not heard shall understand. [22]On which account also I was being hindered, for the most part, from coming to you. [23]Now, however, I have no longer place in these parts, but have still, after many years, a great desire to come to you [24]whenever I take my journey into Spain: for I hope in passing through to see you, and to be forwarded by you on my way thither, if I should first have had some measure of enjoyment of you. [25]But now I go to Jerusalem, ministering to the saints. [26]For Macedonia and Achaia have thought good to make a certain contribution for the poor of the saints in Jerusalem. [27]For besides that they thought good to do so, they are their debtors. For if the gentiles have participated in their spiritual things, they also ought to minister to them in carnal things. [28]When therefore, I have performed this, and sealed to them this fruit, I will go by you into Spain. [29]And I know that when I come to you, I shall come in the fulness of the blessing of Christ. [30]Now I beseech you, brethren, by our Lord Jesus Christ, and by the love of the Spirit, to strive with me in prayers to God in my behalf; [31]that I may be delivered from them in Judæa who believe not, and that the ministration I have for Jerusalem may be acceptable to the saints: [32]that I may come to you in joy by the will of God, and may be refreshed together with you. [33]The God of peace be with with you all. Amen.

XVI. ¹I commend to you Phœbe our sister, who is a deaconess of the church at Cenchreæ; ²that ye may receive her in the Lord in a manner worthy of saints, and assist her in whatever matter she may have need of you: for she, on her part, has been a succourer of many, and of myself. ³Salute Prisca and Aquila, my fellow-workers in Christ Jesus,—⁴who for my life submitted their own necks; to whom not only I give thanks, but also all the churches of the gentiles—⁵and the church that is in their house. Salute Epænetus, my beloved, who is the first-fruits of Asia unto Christ. ⁶Salute Mary, who bestowed much labour on us. ⁷Salute Andronicus and Junias, my kinsmen, and my fellow-prisoners, who are of note among the apostles, who also were in Christ before me. ⁸Salute Amplias, my beloved in the Lord. ⁹Salute Urbanus, my fellow-worker in Christ, and Stachys my beloved. ¹⁰Salute Apelles, approved in Christ. Salute them who are of the household of Aristobulus. ¹¹Salute Herodion, my kinsman. Salute them who are of the household of Narcissus, who are in the Lord. ¹²Salute Tryphœna and Tryphosa, who labour in the Lord. Salute Persis, the beloved, who laboured much in the Lord. ¹³Salute Rufus, chosen in the Lord, and the mother of him and of me. ¹⁴Salute Asyncritus, Phlegon, Hermes, Patrobas, Hermas, and the brethren with them. ¹⁵Salute Philologus and Julia, Nereus and his sister, and Olympas, and all the saints with them. ¹⁶Salute one another with a holy kiss. All the churches of Christ salute you.

¹⁷Now I beseech you, brethren, to mark them who cause divisions and offences, in opposition to the doctrine which ye learnt; and avoid them. ¹⁸For they that are such serve not our Lord Christ, but their own belly; and by good words and fair speeches deceive the hearts of the simple. ¹⁹For your obedience has gone abroad unto all men. I rejoice, therefore, over you: but I would have you be wise as to what is good, and harmless as to what is evil. ²⁰And the God of peace will bruise Satan under your feet shortly. The grace of our Lord Jesus Christ be with you.

²¹Timotheus, my fellow-worker, salutes you, as do also Lucius, and Jason, and Sosipater, my kinsmen. ²²I Tertius, who wrote

the Epistle, salute you in the Lord. ²³Gaius, my host and the host of the whole church, salutes you. Erastus, the treasurer of the city, salutes you; also Quartus, a brother.

²⁴To Him who is able to stablish you, according to my gospel and the preaching of Jesus Christ according to the revelation of the mystery which has been kept secret through eternal times, ²⁵but is now manifested, and by the prophetic scriptures, according to the ordinance of the eternal God, made known to all nations for the obedience of faith—²⁶the only wise God—through Jesus Christ: to Whom be glory to the ages of ages. Amen.

NOTES.

(N.B. A.V. is an abbreviation for Authorized Version, and R.A.V. for the Revision by "Five Clergymen.")

CHAPTER I. 4. Τοῦ ὁρισθέντος, 'determined,' or 'ordained.' This sense of ὁρίζω occurs in other passages of the N. T., as especially in Acts x. 42 and xvii. 31. The translation 'declared' is without support from any other passage. Ἐξ ἀναστάσεως νεκρῶν, 'from,' or 'because of the resurrection of the dead.' The preposition ἐκ has this signification in Acts xxviii. 3, and in Rev. viii. 13. The interpretation of the passage appears to be, that Jesus Christ was ordained Son of God in power by reason of the resurrection of the dead, which was foreordained, and of which, he as Son of God, is destined to be the author. He said himself, "I am the resurrection and the life." (Joh. xi. 25.) Consequently 'in power' is to be taken in strict connection with 'the resurrection,' the power being that which will be preeminently unfolded in the judgment consequent upon the resurrection.

5. Ὑπακοὴν πίστεως, 'the obedience of faith,' that is, obedience proceeding from and qualified by faith, which, therefore, might be called 'faith obedience.' For this reason there is no article before ὑπακοήν.

8. Πρῶτον, 'first of all,' that is, before entering upon the main purpose of the Epistle. The translation should be 'I first thank,' not 'First, I thank'; for this would imply that 'secondly' follows, which is not the case. Περὶ, 'concerning' or 'respecting.' The Cod. Sinait. has περὶ in place of ὑπέρ.

10. Εὐοδόομαι is used in the general sense of 'prospering' or 'being successful,' without particular reference to a journey, as 'good-speed' is used in English. The context shews that ἤδη ποτὲ means 'at some indefinite future time,' or, in English idiom, 'at length.'

12. Τοῦτο δέ ἐστι differs from τουτέστι, the particle δέ being significant. I have translated accordingly.

15. Οὕτω, 'in this way,' that is, because he is debtor &c., and therefore nearly equivalent to 'hence.' Τὸ κατ' ἐμὲ πρόθυμον, 'the readiness that is in me,' quod in me promtum est. *Vulg.* This refers to the desire of the Apostle expressed in v. 11, and implicitly to his being hindered from effecting his purpose.

17. The righteousness of God is revealed in the Gospel to be from faith, because antecedent reception and belief of the Gospel are required for understanding and attaining to the righteousness which is acceptable to God (see Rom. ix. 30—33 and x. 2, 3). 'From faith unto faith' means from one degree of faith to another, according to a form of expression used by St Paul

again in vi. 19. That faith is capable of increase may be proved from Luke xvii. 5, 6, and from 2 Thess. i. 3. The higher the degree of faith the better will God's righteousness be understood. It is evident that ὁ δίκαιος ἐκ πίστεως must be taken together, because this passage is quoted from Habakkuk (ii. 4) expressly to justify the formula ἡ δικαιοσύνη ἐκ πίστεως.

18. 'The revelation from heaven' is put in contrast with the revelation in the Gospel, the latter being the revelation of God's righteousness in them that believe, whereby they are made meet for eternal life; and the other the revelation of God's righteous wrath in the day when He judges the sins of all men. This manifestation of righteousness is a necessary complement of the other, because without it the *whole* of God's righteousness is not unfolded. This accounts for the 'for' at the beginning of v. 18.

20. 'Things invisible from the creation of the world' expresses that the things are such that they never have been, nor can be, objects of sense. For instance abstract realities, such as power and godhead, can be understood only by means of experience and observation of the external world. This passage of St Paul distinctly asserts that objects of sense, furnished by God's creation, are the necessary antecedents of abstract conceptions.

21. Ἐματαιώθησαν ἐν τοῖς διαλογισμοῖς αὐτῶν, 'they were frustrated in their reasonings,' or 'through foolishness reasoned to no purpose.' In the adopted translation I have preferred 'empty' to 'vain,' because the latter word is now generally used in the sense of 'ostentatious.'

22. Φάσκοντες εἶναι σοφοί, 'asserting that they are wise,' 'claiming to be wise.'

23. Ἐν ὁμοιώματι εἰκόνος, 'in' or 'into a likeness by an image,' εἰκόνος being a genitive of quality governed by ἐκ understood, so that the expression might be rendered 'into an image-likeness.' The genitive φθαρτοῦ ἀνθρώπου depends on ὁμοιώματι, and is so rendered in A.V. In R.A.V. it is made to depend on εἰκόνος.

24. The καὶ before παρέδωκεν is not in Cod. Sinait. Διό, 'on account of which,' refers exclusively to the idolatry spoken of just before, and for this reason v. 24 is put between dashes, to indicate that it is parenthetical. At the end of the verse the reading of the more ancient MSS., inclusive of the Cod. Sinait., is ἐν αὐτοῖς in place of ἐν ἑαυτοῖς. The translation 'among themselves' is, however, admissible, the verb ἀτιμάζεσθαι being taken in a middle sense.

25. The antecedent of the relative ὅστις is generally more indefinite, or more remote, than that of ὅς. Here οἵτινες has for its antecedent all respecting whom the previous assertions are made.

26. Διὰ τοῦτο, 'therefore,' here points to a *general* inference from the foregoing statements, and is accordingly put at the beginning of a paragraph.

28. Οὐκ ἐδοκίμασαν ἔχειν, 'did not think good to have,' or 'did not approve having.' Ἀδόκιμος, *improbus*, reprobate. The adopted translation exhibits the etymological relation in the original between δοκιμάζω and ἀδόκιμος.

30. Θεοστυγεῖς, 'haters of God.' In R. A. V. 'hated of God,' which is the pagan meaning of the word. But θεοσεβής is 'a worshipper of God,' θεοσυλής 'a plunderer of God'; then why not θεοστυγής 'a hater of God'?

32. Οἵτινες, 'who,' embracing all the classes of sinners previously men-

tioned. See note on I. 25. This instance seems to shew that the signification 'inasmuch as they,' attributed to this relative pronoun by Alford in v. 25, is inadmissible.

CHAPTER II. 3—5. Verses 3 and 4 ought certainly to be taken affirmatively, the affirmations being of the same kind as "thou that judgest doest the same things" in verse 1. There is no reason for taking these verses interrogatively which does not equally apply to verse 5, which clearly cannot be so taken. Moreover it is particularly to be noticed that the Apostle here refers to two distinct classes of persons (as is shewn by the disjunctive particle ἤ at the beginning of verse 4), one consisting of those who in pharisaical self-confidence presume that they enjoy the special favour of God, and that they will not be judged and punished like other men, and the other of those who, disbelieving, like the Sadducees, the reality of the resurrection and the future judgment, are insensible to the forbearance and longsuffering of God, by which opportunity and space are given them for repentance. These classes, as they have existed in past ages, exist also in the present day, in accordance, seemingly, with a general *law* governing the developement of human sinfulness. It may be supposed that St Paul, from the wisdom that was given to him, understood this, and accordingly made the assertions contained in verses 3, 4, and 5.

7. The clause, καθ᾽ ὑπομονὴν ἔργου ἀγαθοῦ, does not signify that the patience, or endurance, with which good works are maintained is the *means* of seeking for glory, honour, and incorruption, but rather the reason of the *hope* which is in them who seek for such things (see Rom. v. 3—5); for plainly no one seeks for any benefit without the hope of obtaining it. According to this interpretation, κατά is not used here in the sense of 'by,' but in the same sense as the preposition 'under' in such expressions as under trials, under difficulties, &c.

8, 9. The nominatives θυμὸς καὶ ὀργή, θλίψις καὶ στενοχωρία, may be accounted for by supposing 'will be' to be understood. The omission of parts of the verb 'to be' is so common in the Greek of the N. T. that in this, as in other instances, I have thought it unnecessary to indicate that the omission is supplied in the translation. In fact, the ellipsis of the substantive verb, which is characteristic of ideal description, must needs be supplied when, for the sake of the English reader, the writing is put into the narrative or affirmative form.

12. The aorist ἥμαρτον is here used not narratively, but in an abstract, or general sense, the affirmations embracing ideally all who sin, whether in past, present, or future time. According to English idiom this aorist should be rendered by a present, or by a perfect past. (See the Introduction.) As according to the subsequent doctrine of the Apostle all are under either the law of conscience, or the written law, and all will be judged through law, this verse must be understood to state the consequence of the alternative supposition, that any sin without law. If such there be, they will perish, not being capable, without law, of being judged.

13. Here we have a distinct assertion that justification consists of actual and personal righteousness. So St John (1 Ep. iii. 7), "Little

children, let no one deceive you; he that doeth righteousness is righteous, as He [Christ] is righteous."

15, 16. To put verses 13—15 in parentheses, as is done in A. V., or, what is equivalent, to put a colon at the end of verse 15, as is done by the "Five Clergymen," involves the assumption that St Paul's writing was unlike that of any other writer; which there is no ground for assuming. According to ordinary syntax, verse 16 goes on consecutively from verse 15, the latter verse describing the working of the law of conscience in the day of judgment in those who were not under the written law, and the two verses taken together affirming that their thoughts in that day, one with another, thought with thought, accuse, or also excuse. (For the sense of ἢ καί, see Luke xii. 21 and Rom. iv. 9.). This translation accounts for τὰ κρυπτά. Also 'according to my gospel' is exemplified, as respects the judgment, by the gospel which St Paul preached to the Athenians (Acts xvii. 31). Theodoret, in his Commentary, takes verses 15 and 16 as both referring to the future judgment (τὸ μέλλον κριτήριον).

17. The reading Εἰ δὲ of the Cod. Sinait., and of the older MSS. generally, is undoubtedly correct. The substitution of ἴδε in the received text is incompatible with the Apostle's argument, and shews how extensively it has been misunderstood. For hitherto Jew and Gentile have been alike addressed, as is proved by the words, ὦ ἄνθρωπε πᾶς ὁ κρίνων, in verse 1. What follows is addressed specially to the Jew.

21—23. These clauses, taken affirmatively, are in accordance with the doctrine taught in verses 1, 3, 4, and 5. If they are taken interrogatively, the γὰρ which introduces the quotation in v. 24 does not appear to admit of being accounted for.

24. This quotation from Is. lii. 5 (as given in the Septuagint), proves from *Scripture* that the Jew, is not, as Jew, exempt from sin. The force of the argument depends on the coincidence of Scripture with matter of fact. An appeal simply to facts would not have had the same authority.

26. Both ἡ ἀκροβυστία and ἡ περιτομὴ are used personally as well as impersonally. (See Eph. ii. 11.) Also it seems that each may signify either a single person, or persons collectively. Alford, on Phil. iii. 5, maintains that περιτομὴ is only used collectively. But the nominative case in that passage is not without the authority of MSS., and may possibly have been changed to the dative on account of a supposed difficulty in translating it. The context of Col. iii. 11, appears to indicate that περιτομὴ and ἀκροβυστία may designate individuals, and the passage before us almost necessitates this conclusion with respect to the latter word. I have translated accordingly.

29. It is not meant that praise is rendered by God, but that the praiseworthiness, or honour, that belongs to circumcision of the heart is from God.

CHAPTER III. 2. Neither here, nor in Chap. i. 8, is there any anacoluthon, as supposed by Alford, who says that the Apostle begins with πρῶτον with the intention, not subsequently fulfilled, of proceeding to secondly, &c. But in the latter passage, as already intimated, πρῶτον indicates that he begins with what is preliminary to the main subject; and in the present passage the same word is to be taken in the not unusual sense of 'chiefly' or 'principally.' The adopted translation follows A. V. in this respect; I have only added 'indeed,' in order to translate more exactly the expression πρῶτον μὲν γάρ. The particle γὰρ, which merely indicates that what follows is explanatory of the antecedent assertion, is sufficiently taken account of by this translation together with the punctuation. The same expression occurs in 1 Cor. xi. 18, where for like reasons it may be translated in the same manner.

3. It is singular that the formula τί γάρ; is not noticed in Matthiæ's Greek Grammar, although it frequently occurs in the Classics, as well as in the Scriptures. I have collected the following instances:—Phil. i. 16; Job iv. 17, vi. 5 and 22, xv. 7, xvi. 3, xxi. 4, in all which τί γάρ; precedes a question asked by μή as in the present instance; Euripides (Matthiæ), *Suppl.* 48, *Iphig. in Tauris*, 803; Æschylus (Blomf.), *Agam.* 263; Xenophon (Schneider), *Cyri Discipl.* I. 6. 12, where the formula begins a paragraph, v. 2. 27 (see Schneider's note), v. 5. 18 and 19, *Memorab.* III. 10. 3. From these examples it may with certainty be gathered that τι γάρ; is a *transition* formula, used to dismiss what goes before, and to call attention to what follows, and that it may in general be translated, What now?* Accordingly in the present instance, it shews that verse 3 has no immediate relation to verses 1 and 2, and, in consequence, I have supposed it to begin a fresh paragraph, and to introduce a new subject. This subject is *unbelief* (ἀπιστία), the relation of which to God's righteousness the Apostle proceeds to argue upon. Εἰ ἠπίστησάν τινες, 'if some men have not believed,' is equivalent to saying, if unbelief has existed in the world; because unbelief exists whoever they are that disbelieve, and whether they be many or few. [The reasons for translating the aorist by a perfect past are given in the Introduction.] Τὴν πίστιν τοῦ θεοῦ, 'the faithfulness of God,' on which the faith of man rests, and without which it does not exist. So far, therefore, as men disbelieve, the faithfulness of God would seem to be without effect.

4. I have thought it best to give to the formula μὴ γένοιτο a more literal rendering than 'God forbid,' which is open to the objection that it brings in the divine name where it does not occur in the original. By the particular form given to the phrase, the direct expression of a negative was avoided, and in like manner σὺ εἶπας,. 'thou sayest,' was used in place of a direct affirmative. (See Matth. xxvi. 25 and 64.) As these formulæ are indicative of modes of thought or feeling prevailing at the time, it is proper to express them in a translation. It seems to me that the rendering of the phrase by 'May it not be!' with a note of exclamation, expresses both the character of the negation, and the indefiniteness of the nominative to γένοιτο. This, accordingly, has been done.

---

* Τί οὖν; and Τί γάρ; differ in this respect: the former refers to what goes before, because οὖν is used in drawing an inference, and the latter to what follows, because γάρ is used in giving a reason. Hence as τί οὖν; is translated, 'what then?' on the same principle τί γάρ; may be translated, 'what now?'

The Apostle, after repudiating by this negative the previous inference, argues that those who are liars (i.e. sinful because of unbelief), while God is true (i.e. righteous because of His faithfulness), are brought into judgment in order that thereby God's righteousness might be declared and established.

5. Here it is admitted, in accordance with the previous statement, that man's unrighteousness is a necessary antecedent condition of the visible unfolding of God's righteousness, the verb συνίστημι not having the remote meaning 'commends,' but the more primitive meaning, 'constitutes,' or 'makes.' Hence arises the very natural question, If this be so, is not God unrighteous in the wrathful punishment (τὴν ὀργὴν) which He will inflict in the day of judgment? The expression κατὰ ἄνθρωπον λέγω in parentheses intimates that the question is put from a human point of view.

6. After deprecating (by the formula μὴ γένοιτο) the drawing of such an inference, the Apostle meets the question by another, viz., How without punishment can God judge the world? For clearly judging offenders is of no avail unless there be award of punishment. Thus it is evident that St Paul's argument wholly turns on the doctrine that the future judgment is alike demanded for the manifestation of the glory of God, and for the eternal good of man. This accounts for his saying 'according to my gospel' in ii. 16, where he is speaking of events that take place in the day of judgment.

7 and 8. Instead of Εἰ γὰρ at the beginning of v. 7, several MSS., and among them the Cod. Sinait., have Εἰ δέ. The latter reading seems most suitable to the course of the reasoning, the previous argument having applied to the world in general, and a new argument here commencing which is exclusively applicable to the "saints," whether Jews or Gentiles, to whom the Epistle is addressed. This is proved by κἀγὼ in v. 7, and by the verbs in the first person plural in v. 8. The Apostle, after admitting the doctrine just established, viz. that the truth (or righteousness) of God abounds in the lie (or sin) of man to His glory, and taking it as applicable to himself equally with others, asks, Why am even I (κἀγὼ) judged as a sinner? [It should be noticed that 'truth' (ἀλήθεια) and 'lie' (ψεῦσμα) are here specific terms for general, just as ἀληθὴς and ψεύστης were in v. 4.] It is plain that St Paul asks this question as being one among the number of those who are entitled to the designation of "called saints;" for he passes immediately from the first person singular to the first person plural, and thus identifies himself with those he is writing to, whom he addresses under that designation. The question, therefore, amounts to this: Why are those who are called out of the world by the favour of God judged as sinners? Then follows a *second* question, different from the other, but equally arising out of the previous doctrine respecting the manner in which God's righteousness is manifested. Why, it is asked, if man's unrighteousness is necessarily antecedent to the developement of God's righteousness, should not we, to whom this doctrine is made known, do evil things that the good things resulting from righteous judgment may come? This question appears to be put in the very terms which the blasphemers made use of to distort the Apostle's doctrine: ποιήσωμεν τὰ κακά, ἵνα ἔλθῃ τὰ ἀγαθὰ ὧν τὸ κρίμα

ἔνδικόν ἐστι. The antecedent of ὧν being τὰ ἀγαθὰ, it follows that ὧν τὸ κρίμα signifies 'the judgment of good things.' This expression may be taken in the same sense as "the judgments of thy righteousness" (τὰ κρίματα τῆς δικαιοσύνης σου), in Ps. cxix. 7, it being understood from the antecedent argument that the unfolding of God's righteousness is the end of creation, and the consummation of His own glory and man's good. Hence 'the good things of which the judgment is just' might be a perverse mode of saying, 'the good effects of the righteousness established by God's righteous judgment.' There can, I think, be no doubt that τὸ κρίμα ought not to be translated 'damnation' as in A.V., or by its equivalent 'condemnation,' as in R.A.V., this being specially the meaning of κατάκριμα. Also according to ordinary syntax the antecedent of ὧν can be no other than τὰ ἀγαθά. Besides, it does not appear, if τινες be taken to be the antecedent, how the *obiter* assertion, that the judgment of the blasphemers is just, can have any bearing upon the argument. The obscurity of this very difficult passage seems to me to be removed by the proposed translation and interpretation. It would appear from Jerome's Version, as edited by Tischendorf from the Codex Amiatinus, that at an early date the whole passage, iii. 3—9, was misinterpreted, and that St Paul's doctrine and gospel therein contained were misunderstood.

9. It is particularly to be noticed that the answer to the *first* of the two preceding questions is here entered upon without reference to the other, the answer to which is deferred to chap. vi. I have, therefore, put 'What then?' (Τί οὖν;), which introduces the answer, at the beginning of a paragraph. From the explanation above given of the purport of the first question it may be inferred that 'do we excel?' (προεχόμεθα;) signifies, 'are we, who have been called, better than others?' The apostle replies to this enquiry, 'we are in no respect better,' and, accordingly, his answer to the first question is equivalent to saying that the saints are judged because they like others have sinned. Similar doctrine is taught in 2 Cor. v. 10.

To substantiate the position that all are equally sinners, reference is first made to a previous argument to that effect (προητιασάμεθα), embracing both Jews and Gentiles, viz. that contained in chap. i. 20—32 and chap. ii. 1—24, which argument, so far as it relates to the Jew, is supported by a single quotation (in ii. 24) from Scripture. Then for farther confirmation of the doctrine of universal sin the Apostle quotes from the Scriptures much more largely.

10—19. This series of quotations, taken from various parts of the Psalms, for the most part as given in the Septuagint, prove the universality of sin without *any* exception, the statements being applicable to all Jews inasmuch as they are contained in their own Scriptures. In *v.* 19 ὁ νόμος means the whole of the Jewish Scriptures (see Alford *in loc.*).

23 and 24. The verb ὑστεροῦνται signifies that all not merely 'come short of,' but are originally 'wholly destitute of' that which constitutes the glory of God, viz. the righteousness which He bestows on His redeemed people. Hence the Apostle goes on to say, "being justified freely by His grace through the redemption which is in Christ Jesus." It is to be understood that this justification, though it is free and of grace, consists of *personal*

righteousness, as is made plain by doctrine taught in a subsequent part of the Epistle. "The redemption in Christ Jesus" is described in Tit. ii. 14 in these terms: "Who gave himself for us that he might redeem us from all iniquity, and purify for himself a peculiar people zealous of good works."

25 and 26. Here we are taught that God, who, as being a God of righteousness is necessarily offended by the sins of men, has Himself set forth a propitiation for sin (i. e. a means of reconciliation) in the death of His Son Jesus Christ. [ἐν τῷ αὐτοῦ αἵματι can only mean 'in his death.'] The death of Christ operates in this way because it consummated his manifestation (ἔνδειξιν) of God's righteousness, and thus became the special object of that faith which is the antecedent of actual and personal righteousness like that of Christ, and without which it is impossible to please God (Heb. xi. 6). This explains why the propitiation is "through faith." Without such righteousness from faith there cannot be reconciliation with an offended God. This mode of propitiation arises out of that law of our spiritual creation according to which all are made sinners by the law before they are made righteous by grace, it not being possible for any one to attain to righteousness except by remission of *antecedent* sins. The clause, διὰ τὴν πάρεσιν τῶν προγεγονότων ἁμαρτημάτων, 'on account of the remission of antecedent sins,' implies that such remission was a foreordained part of the plan of redemption. For this reason our Lord said, "I came not to call the righteous, but sinners" (Matth. ix. 13). For the sake of the remission of sins space is given for repentance, as is signified by the clause, ἐν τῇ ἀνοχῇ τοῦ θεοῦ, 'in the forbearance of God.' Also it is evident that this plan necessitates 'the shewing forth' of that righteousness of God which those partake of, through faith, whose sins are remitted. But this manifestation of God's righteousness differs from that which will take place in the great day of judgment, inasmuch as it has been accomplished in the present age of the world (ἐν τῷ νῦν καιρῷ), in order that God might be shewn to be just while He makes just him who is of the faith of Jesus. This passage, so full of meaning, is a kind of epitome of St Paul's doctrine.

28. Although faith is the antecedent of righteousness 'apart from works of the law' (χωρὶς ἔργων νόμου), it does not follow that the righteousness is not *actual*. It is *doing* the works in consequence of the gift of faith.

29. Probably the strict translation of 'Η Ἰουδαίων ὁ θεὸς μόνον; is, 'Does God pertain to the Jews only?' and that of οὐχὶ καὶ ἐθνῶν; 'not to the Gentiles also?'

30. '*From* faith' (ἐκ πίστεως) indicates the *law* of the antecedence of faith to righteousness; '*through* faith' (διὰ τῆς πίστεως) signifies that faith is the *means* of attaining to righteousness.

31. The moral law is established 'through faith,' because faith has its proper effect in the fulfilment of the righteousness of the law (see Rom. viii. 4). It would certainly appear from this passage that St Paul had in mind no other justification by faith than actual and personal righteousness.—The expression μὴ γένοιτο might here be simply translated 'nay,' or 'not so,' on account of ἀλλὰ following. After a negation ἀλλὰ not unfrequently signifies *sed potius*. (See Schleusner in voc.)

CHAPTER IV. 1. 'According to flesh' (κατὰ σάρκα) means 'outwardly,' 'visibly,' nearly in the same sense as ἐξ ἔργων in the next verse. Theodoret remarks on this place:—κατὰ σάρκα τὴν ἐν ἔργοις λέγει· ἐπειδήπερ διὰ τοῦ σώματος ἐκπληροῦμεν τὰ ἔργα.

2. St Paul here refers to the doctrine that 'Abraham was justified from works' as if it were generally acknowledged, and admitted of no question. The conjunction εἰ with the indicative mood is not used in a conditional sense, but, generally, for making an *allowable supposition*. The Apostle's argument is of this kind: What then has Abraham obtained by outward act? For supposing, as is admitted to be true, that he was justified from works, then according to the previous argument (iii. 27), boasting would not be excluded. This dilemma is met by saying that as regards God there is no ground for boasting. The Apostle then proceeds (in *v.* 3) to maintain this position by argument from Scripture.

I take this occasion to remark that the doctrine of Abraham's justification by works is expressed here by St Paul in the same terms as those employed by St James (ii. 23, 24), and the same passage of Genesis (xv. 6) is quoted by both. It appears, therefore, that the views of these two Apostles respecting the doctrine of *justification* differed in no respect. As they were enlightened by the same Spirit, it is not possible that they should have regarded in an essentially different manner a fundamental doctrine of Christianity. The assertion, so confidently made by some in these days, that the doctrine of St Paul concerning justification is irreconcileable with that of St James, has no other foundation than a misunderstanding of what is meant by the faith of a believer being reckoned to him unto righteousness. This will be made plain by the remarks which follow.

3. The doctrine that faith is reckoned unto righteousness involves two distinct considerations: first, that faith, according to a *law* which God has ordained, *precedes* (as is shewn by the expression "*unto* righteousness") the righteousness which consists in doing good works that are pleasing to God; and secondly, that together with that law, God also ordained that the righteousness which is consequent upon faith shall be a *benefit* to the believer. Hence the word "reckon" is used to shew that faith and righteousness are related not merely as antecedent and consequent, but that there is *profit* in the relation. For, in fact, to be complete in righteousness is man's greatest good and the perfection of his nature, and therefore what contributes to that end is said to be reckoned, as a sum of money is reckoned to any one's advantage. Thus St Peter (2 Ep. i. 1) speaks of faith being "precious in righteousness," meaning that it is to be accounted of value because it has its appropriate effect in righteousness.

But with respect to this doctrine of righteousness from faith, it is particularly to be understood that faith is that spiritual gift the quality of which is defined in Heb. xi. 1; that is, it consists of an intelligent comprehension of the promised good things of the life to come, united with a well-founded hope of partaking of them. There is no such thing as a saving faith without a distinct recognition and hope of the future life. Hope sustains the faithful under the trial and suffering of well doing (ii. 8), and therefore by hope they are saved (viii. 24).

4 and 5. This passage indicates clearly the meaning of the word "reckon" (λογίζομαι), as applied in the doctrine of justification by faith. It shews that the reckoning of faith unto righteousness is an actual and substantial benefit to the believer, just like the benefit to a workman of the payment he receives for his work; but there is this difference, that whereas the workman can claim his wages as a debt, he that "believes on Him who justifies the ungodly" does not thereby acquire any claim to the reward of righteousness, for both the righteousness and the antecedent faith are altogether of grace (see Eph. ii. 8).

6—8. The foregoing doctrine is finally confirmed by a quotation from one of the Psalms of David, in which the Psalmist pronounces those to be happy "whose iniquities are forgiven and whose sins are covered" (Ps. xxxii. 1, 2). In making this citation the Apostle intimates that they whose sins are forgiven are identical with those "to whom God reckons righteousness apart from works;" for, in fact, the bestowal of the gift of righteousness in consequence of faith, and without taking account of works done before faith, is both the means and the evidence of the forgiveness of sins. They whose sins are forgiven are "blessed" by reason of that reckoning unto righteousness. In short, the form of the reference to the authority of David (in *v.* 6) clearly shews that the passage is cited because the word μακάριος (blessed), occurring in it twice, exemplifies the sense in which the word λογίζεται (is reckoned) is to be taken in the Apostle's doctrine of justification by faith.

10. I have added 'to him' because of ὄντι in the next clause.

11. No punctuation is required after 'believe through uncircumcision,' these words being immediately connected with those following.

16. From the tenor of the antecedent argument it may be inferred that the ellipsis before ἐκ πίστεως, 'of faith,' and that before κατὰ χάριν, 'according to grace,' are intended to fix attention on these two formulæ as expressing *laws* of man's spiritual creation. It is, therefore, unnecessary to supply 'the inheritance,' as proposed by the "Five Clergymen," the character of the Apostle's teaching being best conveyed by not filling up the ellipses.

19 and 20. As οὐ before κατενόησεν is omitted in the Cod. Sinait. and other of the early MSS., and as this omission agrees best with the copula καὶ before τὴν νέκρωσιν, I have translated accordingly. The δέ at the beginning of *v.* 20 is consequently adversative, and may be translated 'yet.' Since in A. V. διακρινόμενος in Jam. i. 6 is translated 'wavering,' the rendering of οὐ διεκρίθη here by 'did not waver,' seems preferable to 'staggered not.'

Τῇ ἀπιστίᾳ, 'through' or 'by reason of unbelief,' τῇ πίστει, 'by faith,' nearly as in xi. 20, faith having the property of strengthening and confirming.

25. The preposition διὰ ought clearly to have the same translation and the same meaning before τὴν δικαίωσιν as before τὰ παραπτώματα. In the A. V. it is in both cases translated 'for;' but the meaning of one 'for' is not the same as that of the other. In fact, it is hard to perceive in what way Christ was delivered up *for* our offences. I have adopted the ordinary rendering, 'on account of,' of διὰ with the accusative; but the saying that Jesus Christ 'was raised on account of our justification,' must be understood to imply that justification through his death and resurrection was antecedently determined upon in the counsels of the Almighty.

CHAPTER V. 1. After establishing the doctrine of righteousness from faith St Paul proceeds to state the chief spiritual effects of this justification. These are, peace (*v.* 1), joy (*vv.* 2 and 3), hope (*v.* 4), love (*v.* 5). In Gal. v. 22, the fruit of the Spirit, is said to consist of "love, joy, peace," with other spiritual affections, among which faith (πίστις) is mentioned, but not hope. But, in truth, these two spiritual gifts are so closely related that one may be considered to involve the other. (See at the end of the remarks on iv. 3.) The various spiritual affections enumerated in that passage of the Epistle to the Galatians constitute *sanctification*, as distinct from, and consequent upon, justification. This is what St Paul calls "fruit of [or from] righteousness"(καρπὸν δικαιοσύνης) in Phil. i. 11. Also St James (iii. 18) has the more explicit expression "fruit from righteousness in peace" (καρπὸς δικαιοσύνης ἐν εἰρήνῃ), with which may be compared the very similar expression "yields peaceable fruit from righteousness" (καρπὸν εἰρηνικὸν ἀποδίδωσι δικαιοσύνης) in Heb xii. 11. [As καρπὸς εἰρηνικὸς is equivalent to καρπὸς ἐν εἰρήνῃ, this passage shews that the insertion of "is sown" before "in peace" in the authorized translation of Jam. iii. 18 is incorrect]. The rendering of Eph. v. 9 in A. V., viz. 'The fruit of the Spirit is in ...... righteousness...,' might seem to contradict this view of the relation of sanctification to justification. But in place of πνεύματος the Cod. Sinait. and other ancient MSS. have φωτός, which instead of contradicting is rather confirmatory of the foregoing explanations.

Hence I think we may conclude on doctrinal grounds that ἔχομεν is the true reading in the passage before us, although ἔχωμεν is strongly supported by MSS. In the Cod. Sinait. the latter reading is corrected into ἔχομεν by an early hand. The "Five Clergymen" have adopted the subjunctive form, and consequently translate in a hortatory sense; but Alford (*in loc.*) argues well in defence of the indicative.

2. I have taken καυχώμεθα in the sense of 'rejoice,' because, according to the commentary on *v.* 1, joy is one of the principal fruits of the Spirit.

4. Δοκιμὴ signifies inward 'experience,' not 'approval' from without, all the affections here mentioned being *spiritual.* If it signifies 'inward approval' the translation 'experience' is sufficiently exact, and is free from ambiguity.

7. The γὰρ in the second clause of this verse indicates that this clause assigns a reason for the word 'scarcely' (μόλις) in the first, namely, that it cannot be said without qualification that no one would die for a righteous man, because in behalf of that which is good some one might be found willing even to die. I take τοῦ ἀγαθοῦ to be of the neuter gender in accordance with other instances that will subsequently come under consideration, in which St. Paul expresses by the neuter gender general, or abstract truths. Besides, it would otherwise be hard to account for the article being before ἀγαθοῦ and not before δικαίου.

8. The sense of συνίστησι here appears to be, 'establishes by external manifestation,' or, more briefly expressed, 'makes manifest.'

9. Here, as in other instances, ἡ ὀργὴ is specifically 'the wrath' revealed in the future judgment.

11. The "Five Clergymen" translate τὴν καταλλαγὴν 'our reconciliation,' although the article only serves to refer to the reconciliation just before mentioned, and there is no pronoun in the Greek.

12. The apostle here commences an explanation of the reason that sin and death are in the world, founded on the previous doctrine of justification by faith, and reconciliation to God through Jesus Christ. To indicate this the paragraph begins with Διὰ τοῦτο, 'on this account,' or 'for this reason.'

In the A. V. a colon is placed at the end of v. 12, and verses 13—17 are put within parentheses, as if the sense went on continuously from v. 12 to v. 18. The "Five Clergymen" have removed the parentheses, but as they retain the colon, they admit an anacoluthon at the end of v. 12, and, therefore, do not really give a different version from that of A. V. It is not possible that St Paul, or any other intelligent writer, could have written in the way thus represented. To attribute such writing to any author is only giving evidence that his diction, or his subject, is misunderstood. I think I can distinctly point out the source of the misapprehension in this instance. It requires only a moderate acquaintance with the language of the Septuagint to be aware that the particle καὶ is frequently used, not as a copula, but *to indicate the beginning of the apodosis of a sentence*. In the present passage the καὶ before οὕτως performs this part, answering, in fact, the same purpose as punctuation in modern writing. (See the Introduction on this philological question.) When καὶ is thus used, its signification may generally be rendered by punctuation. Frequently, however, it may be translated by 'also' at the beginning of the clause, as I have done in this instance. It follows from these considerations that the apodosis which begins with καὶ οὕτως may be supposed to terminate at the end of v. 12, where, as the sense is complete, there should be a full stop.

The literal translation of ἐφ' ᾧ πάντες ἥμαρτον is, 'for that all sinned,' each sin of each individual being looked upon as an objective fact, which may be spoken of narratively, whether it occurs in time past, present, or future. Hence to the English reader 'all have sinned,' as in A. V., better conveys the meaning of the original than either 'all sinned' or 'all were sinners.' But according to the mode of thought and expression of the present day the sense of the original is given still more truly by the translation 'all sin'; which accordingly is adopted. (See the Introduction.)

14. The phrase ἐπὶ τῷ ὁμοιώματι is strictly 'in likeness' or 'with resemblance,' and may be idiomatically rendered 'after the manner.' 'After the likeness,' in R. A. V., is tautological.

I take τοῦ μέλλοντος to be of the neuter gender, and to signify generally that which was to be afterwards. Adam is a "type of the future" inasmuch as he received an express command, and broke it through temptation from Satan, from the world, consisting of himself and Eve, and from desire of the flesh. His condition, therefore, was like that of all his descendants who have known, and been under, the moral law expressly delivered by God to Moses, and have transgressed it through temptations of which these were typical. The condition of the rest of mankind is different in so far as they received no express command, and have only been under the law of conscience. But sin, that is, the not doing the will of God, was in the world before the promulgation of the law, by reason of that original weakness and imperfection of man's nature, which rendered Adam and Eve incapable of resisting temptation, and which, being transmitted by natural generation, renders all their posterity alike incapable of obedience to the will of God. And although, as regards the future judgment, sin is reckoned only so far as it is a conscious violation of what is known to be right, yet, in virtue of an unalterable *law* of man's spiritual creation, which makes death the consequence of sin, "death reigned from Adam to Moses," as, in truth, it has reigned since, over all who, although they have not broken, as Adam did, a command expressly given by God, have transgressed His laws by reason of inherited frailty and imperfection. This seems to be the explanation of the doctrine (in *v.* 12) that "death passed unto all men for that all sin," and of the subsequent statements in verses 13 and 14.

16. The reading ἁμαρτήματος, which is given in several of the older MSS., although not in the Vatican and the Sinaitic, has been adopted for the following reasons. If we read ἁμαρτήσαντος it will be necessary to take ἐξ ἑνὸς in the next clause to mean 'from one man'; whereas τὸ κρίμα preceding and εἰς κατάκριμα following would seem to shew that ἐξ ἑνὸς must be 'from one sin.' For, in fact, the existence of a single sin against God necessitates both judgment and condemnation. Also according to this interpretation ἐξ ἑνὸς ἁμαρτήματος stands in natural opposition to ἐκ πολλῶν παραπτωμάτων in the next clause.

17. The older MSS. which have ἁμαρτήματος in *v.* 16, with the addition of the Alexandrine, have ἐν ἑνί, or ἐν τῷ ἑνί, in place of τῷ τοῦ ἑνὸς in *v.* 17. I have adopted ἐν ἑνὶ as being apparently demanded by the preceding ἐξ ἑνὸς ἁμαρτήματος.

18. There is no need to fill up the ellipses in this verse, because they are themselves highly significant. We may infer from them that the Apostle has been deducing by argument, and here exhibits in order, the *laws of the spiritual creation* which concern man's destiny, their final causes having already been under consideration in the part of the Epistle which precedes Διὰ τοῦτο in *v.* 12. Similarly with respect to the natural creation there are two kinds of knowledge. By natural science we are able to discover the laws which determine (for instance) day and night, summer and winter, &c.; but it is by the experience of life that we learn what are the final causes of the operation of these laws. Verses 18—21 appear to contain a kind of recapitulation of the whole doctrine, both the part preceding and the part following Διὰ τοῦτο.

19. Sin does not exist but through transgression by the will of man of a divine command. Adam by his disobedience first gave existence to sin, and to a sinful nature, and this by *natural* generation has passed upon all his descendants, as, on the other hand, through the obedience of Jesus Christ the many are made righteous by *spiritual* generation. I understand spiritual generation to consist of the operation of all the means, outward and inward, by which the obedient sons of God are made actual partakers eventually of that perfect righteousness which the obedience of the Son of God unto death gave existence to, which righteousness is called in *v.* 18 δικαίωσις ζωῆς, being the necessary condition of eternal life. These considerations seem to me to be explanatory of the doctrine contained in *v.* 19. It is to be observed that throughout the passage commencing at *v.* 12, "the one" and

"the many" are repeatedly spoken of as mutually related. Also it appears from what is said in v. 18 that "the many" is equivalent to "all men". It seems, therefore, to be a necessary consequence of the apostle's doctrine that the effect of Christ's obedience unto death is coextensive with the effect of Adam's disobedience, and that as all men are made sinners by natural generation, all men will eventually be made righteous by spiritual generation. The present passage does not indicate the particular means by which this great consummation will be brought about, but the future tense "shall be made" (κατασταθήσονται) is significant, and seems to point to the operation of the judgment in the world to come.

20. The statement that the moral law came in, in the course of this dispensation, to the end that sin might be multiplied, is consistent with the whole tenor of the previous argument, which demonstrates that according to the general law of the spiritual creation, the reign of sin and death is antecedent to the evolution, out of the abundance of sins, of the reign of universal and everlasting righteousness.

CHAPTER VI. 1. The authority of the old MSS. is in favour of ἐπιμένωμεν, excepting that the Cod. Sin. has ἐπιμένομεν. The subjunctive seems to be used here in a manner strictly analogous to the English use of 'should' in the sense of 'ought.'

2. Respecting the translation of μὴ γένοιτο see the Note on iii. 4.—The reasons given at the end of the Note on v. 12 for translating the aorist ἥμαρτον by a present, apply here, *mutatis mutandis*, to the translation of ἀπεθάνομεν. The death of each individual is regarded as an objective event which, as it takes place of necessity, may be spoken of historically, whether it belong to past or future time. On this principle the strict translation, 'we who died to sin,' has actually the same general signification as 'we who die to sin;' and since the former might mislead the ordinary English reader, the other, as sufficiently conveying to him the sense of the original, has been adopted. It may here be remarked that the aorist is often used in prophetic writings in speaking of an event that is future (as in Rev. xx. 5), on the principle that what is foretold by the Holy Spirit by whom the prophets spake will surely come to pass.

3. The reference here to the "death" of Christ seems to shew beyond question that "the death to sin" spoken of in the preceding verse is natural death, the death of the body. The Apostle's argument is, that our being subject to *death* on account of sin is a reason for not continuing to *live* in sin. "To die to sin" expresses the law (called in viii. 2 the law of sin and death), according to which sin and mortality are inseparably related. For indicating a relation of this kind, determined by a law of man's spiritual creation, St Paul constantly employs the *dative* case.

4. It appears from what precedes in verse 3 that διὰ τοῦ βαπτίσματος εἰς τὸν θάνατον may be simply translated 'through baptism into death' nearly as in the Authorized Version, both articles being taken to be indefinite. On no intelligible philological principle can the first article be translated by 'our' and the other by 'his,' as is done by the "Five Clergymen." This is not

translation, but an arbitrary limitation of the sense of the original. (See on the usage of the article in the Introduction.)

5. Σύμφυτος is used in classical writers in the sense of συγγενής, which sense is applicable here because Jesus Christ is called "the firstborn among many brethren" (Rom. viii. 29).—It may be supposed that σύμφυτος and συνεσταυρώθη (in v. 6) both govern αὐτῷ understood, this pronoun having been expressed after συνετάφημεν in v. 4. In that case τῷ ὁμοιώματι is a causative dative like the Latin ablative, and both τοῦ θανάτου and τῆς ἀναστάσεως are qualifying genitives.—'Ἀλλὰ καὶ may signify 'moreover' or 'besides,' although οὐ μόνον does not precede. (See Passow under the word ἀλλά.)

6. Τῆς ἁμαρτίας is a genitive of quality, equivalent in English to 'sinful.' This rendering is adopted because the majority of English readers might not readily take 'body of sin' to mean the same as 'sinful body.'

7. This verse contains doctrine of great significance. Expressed in modern language it asserts that the effect of natural death is to free from sin, that is, to justify. The Apostle Peter teaches the same doctrine where he says, "he that has suffered in the flesh has ceased from sin" (1 Pet. iv. 1). By comparison of this passage with that of St Paul we may infer that death, as being the greatest of bodily afflictions, may be taken to include all suffering in the flesh, and that the general effect of suffering is to do away with sin. That suffering in the flesh has such efficacy is proved by the sacrifice of the Son of God, who out of love and sympathy for us in our bondage to "the law of sin and death," endured the evil consequences of that law in their severest form, although he was himself without sin, in order that he might shew to us that the only way to eternal life is through the pains and bitterness of death. Thus although pain and death from one point of view are necessary manifestations of the wrath of a holy God against sin, when viewed in the light of the sufferings of Christ, they are seen to be means of forming the spirits of men for immortality. Otherwise, since our bodies are God's workmanship, we might justly be filled with wonder and perplexity at the many and great evils flesh is heir to. But seeing that the Son of God, in obedience to his Father's will, submitted, by the endurance of sorrow, pain, and death, to laws ordained for the creation of man's spiritual life, what farther proof do we need that the operation of those laws is consistent with the love of a faithful Creator, and that it will eventually issue in eternal life? Even now the understanding and belief of this doctrine of the cross of Christ, by inducing the sinner to cease from sin, effects a *reconciliation* between him and his offended God. (See Rom. v. 11.) Such, I am persuaded, is the doctrine and gospel taught by St Paul in this Epistle; but to those who say that the death he speaks of is any other than the death of the body, this gospel will be entirely hid. The reasoning of the Apostle in verses 2—14 of this sixth Chapter seems expressly intended to shew in what manner mortality, regarded as an incident in man's present existence, operates to prepare him for his final destiny.

8. Respecting the translation of ἀπεθάνομεν by a present tense see the Note on v. 2.

10. The aorist ἀπέθανε is here translated by a present for the same reason

as in verses 2 and 8. Strictly ὁ ἀπέθανε should have no other translation than 'that which died.' But as the English past tense does not, like the Greek aorist, equally apply, whether the event be in past or future time, it is preferable, for the sake of the English reader, to translate 'that which dies.' Farther it should be noticed that the neuter gender of the pronoun ὁ indicates, according to known usage, that the assertion is made abstractedly, or universally. The Apostle refers to the universal characteristic of death, that it takes place at some definite point of time, as is evident from his using the historic aorist, and from the meaning of ἐφάπαξ. On the contrary, with respect to life, which is of a continuous nature, the universal assertion, ὁ ζῇ, ζῇ τῷ θεῷ, is made with the present tense.

11. The signification of λογίσεσθε in this verse is particularly worthy of notice. Having instructed the believing Christians to whom he is writing as to the effect of the law of sin and death, the Apostle, in order to promote their advance in spiritual life, now exhorts them to *reckon themselves* to be already dead by the operation of that law, and to be living to God in Christ Jesus as if they were alive after death (see *v.* 13), inasmuch as they are even now capable of a change of spiritual condition of the same kind as that which, according to the antecedent doctrine, results from the actual experience of death. The word λογίσεσθε consequently proves that the death previously spoken of is death of the body.

12. The Cod. Sin. with other early MSS. has only ταῖς ἐπιθυμίαις αὐτοῦ after εἰς τὸ ὑπακούειν. This reading has been adopted, and αὐτοῦ is rendered 'the body's' in order to avoid the ambiguity (not existing in the Greek) as to the reference of the pronoun 'its' to 'sin' or to 'body.'

13. Schleusner has shewn under the word νεκρὸς that οἱ νεκροὶ is used for θάνατος. This is clearly done on the principle of taking the visible objects 'dead bodies' to represent the more abstract reality 'death.' Hence ὡς ἐκ νεκρῶν ζῶντας may be translated 'as if alive after death.' By the same rule ἀνάστασις ἐκ τῶν νεκρῶν is resurrection after death, and is equivalent to 'resurrection *of* the dead.' But the commonly used expression 'resurrection *from* the dead' has no obvious objective signification, and possibly may have originated from ignorance of the abstract sense of οἱ νεκροί. I take occasion here to remark that according to this usage ἐπὶ νεκροῖς in Heb. ix. 17 is simply 'at decease,' and that the baptism ὑπὲρ τῶν νεκρῶν in 1 Cor. xv. 29 is baptism 'on account of death,' very nearly in the same sense as 'baptism into death' in Rom. vi. 3. The reading ὑπὲρ τῶν νεκρῶν at the end of 1 Cor. xv. 29, hardly to be accounted for unless it were the original reading, may have been changed at an early date into ὑπὲρ αὐτῶν by scribes unacquainted with the abstract meaning of οἱ νεκροί.

16. According to Stephens's *Thesaurus* and other Lexicons ᾧ may be translated *quatenus*, 'so far as;' which appears to be the most appropriate meaning of the first ᾧ in this verse. In classic Greek, however, the feminine dative ᾗ is generally used in this sense. But the neuter dative accords better with the abstract character of the Apostle's reasoning, and at the same time approaches closely in signification to the formula ἐφ' ᾧ in Rom. v. 12, and to ἐν ᾧ in viii. 3. Hence admitting that ᾧ παριστάνετε ἑαυτοὺς may be translated, 'so far as ye yield yourselves,' it will follow that these words refer to

voluntariness as a condition of the service. The expressions 'of sin unto death' and 'of obedience unto righteousness' may be taken to be descriptive of two opposite kinds of service, or servants. But although servants of sin unto death may be said both to serve sin and to be sinful, it can only be said of those who are described as servants of obedience unto righteousness, that they are obedient servants, and not that they serve obedience, this being an incongruous expression.' This consideration shews that although ἁμαρτίας might either be a dependent genitive or a genitive of quality, ὑπακοῆς is necessarily a genitive of quality. Hence the adopted translation of this difficult passage has been made on the supposition that both are genitives of quality.

17. The thanks are given to God not because the Romans had been, but because they ceased to be, servants of sin. This is indicated by the verb ἦτε in the imperfect tense, which implies that they are no longer the servants of sin that they were at one time. I have translated accordingly.

19. Ἡ ἀνομία εἰς τὴν ἀνομίαν is 'iniquity advancing from one degree to a higher.' See the Note on ἐκ πίστεως εἰς πίστιν in i. 17.

20. In this instance ἐλεύθεροι may be translated 'free from service,' because τῇ δικαιοσύνῃ follows in the dative case, this case being specially used, as the context shews, with reference to service. See also Rom. xiv. 4.

CHAPTER VII. 1—4. The argument in this passage rests altogether on the principle that the ordinary laws that govern humanity and human relations, whether as laid down in the Law of Moses, or as established by the customs of nations, were ordained by God, apparently and subordinately, for the support and maintenance of the outward life of individuals and societies, but originally and mainly to be the outward means of giving instruction respecting the formation of man's spiritual life. This was understood by those in the Apostle's day who knew the spirit of the law of Moses; and consequently to establish the doctrine that a man is under subjection to the moral law as long as he lives, it was sufficient to appeal to a typical ordinance of the Jewish law. The ordinance cited is, that a married woman is released from the law of obligation to a husband by his death, so as not to become guilty of sin by marrying another man. Clearly this is an instance in which, abstractedly, *death* sets free from the power of law, and consequently from sin. But these very terms describe the operation by which, according to the doctrine in vi. 7, a man is spiritually justified from sin. (See the note on that passage.) So strict is the analogy that the Apostle argues (in *v.* 4) from the typical case to the other by the inferential particle ὥστε, 'so that,' and proceeds to carry on the analogy a step farther by taking the union, without sin, of the woman with another husband to express the union with Christ of those who, accounting themselves to have already undergone the death due to the law, in that belief "bring forth fruit to God." (See the Note on vi. 11.)

The full meaning of ἐθανατώθητε τῷ νόμῳ is, ye were put to death by the operation of the moral law, which generates, first, sin, and then death. Διὰ τοῦ σώματος τοῦ Χριστοῦ is added, because the death of the Son of God in the flesh on account of the sins of the world involves the death of all men. For

St Paul argues in 2 Cor. v. 14, "we thus judge that if one died for the sake of all, then all die." For as he died on account of their sins to purchase life for them, they die on account of their own sins in order that they may be meet to partake of the life. According to the usual force of ἵνα with the subjunctive aorist, ἵνα καρποφορήσωμεν should be translated, 'that we might bear fruit.' See in v. 13.

6. The true reading is ἀποθανόντες, and τοῦ νόμου is the antecedent of ἐν ᾧ. I have translated accordingly.

7—11. The whole tenor of this argument shews that in using the first person singular St Paul does not describe any special experience of his own, but the personal experience of every believing Christian. We have already had an instance of the same mode of arguing in iii. 7. (See the Note on that passage.) In saying, "I was living once apart from law," he puts a supposable case applicable to any individual, in order to convey distinctly the doctrine that the existence of law is antecedent to the consciousness of sin. That he so argues becomes quite clear when he proceeds to say, "but I died," indicating thus that the suscitation of the power of sin through the commandment is followed by the death of the individual.

As the particle δὲ at the beginnings of verses 8 and 9 appears to have no adversative signification, I consider it to be sufficiently translated by the punctuation. (See the Introduction.)

13. The reading of the older MSS. with Cod. Sin., is ἐγένετο, which has been preferred to γέγονε.

15—21. In these verses I translate ποιῶ 'I do,' πράσσω 'I practise' or 'I do,' and κατεργάζομαι 'I perform,' in order to represent the variety of the words in the original, although they are apparently used in the same sense. —I omit, with Alford, the first τοῦτο in v. 15.—The first ἐγὼ in v. 20 is supported by the Cod. Sin. Since, assuming this to be the true reading, the pronoun must be emphasized, it is here translated 'myself.'—In the translation of v. 21 I have endeavoured to convey the significance of the repetition of ἐμοὶ after τῷ θέλοντι ἐμοὶ in the clause preceding.

24 and 25. Here again, for the reasons already urged, the Apostle does not express by the exclamation "wretched man that I am!" exclusively his own experience, but that of every individual who is struggling to be free from the dominion of the "fleshly lusts that war against the soul" (1 Pet. ii. 11). By such language St Paul represents strongly the destructive power of the desires of the flesh and the misery of being in subjection to them; but that he does not intend thereby to express the normal condition of Christian experience is made evident by his adding, in the same breath as it were, "I am thankful to God through Jesus Christ." A state of thankfulness is not compatible with a state of wretchedness and despair.

Any one familiar with the Greek of the Septuagint, which resembles in so many respects the Greek of the New Testament, would have no difficulty in deciding that ἐκ τοῦ σώματος τοῦ θανάτου τούτου should be translated 'from this body of death,' and not 'from the body of this death,' which is scarcely intelligible. In this syntax τοῦ θανάτου is not a dependent genitive but a genitive of quality, used exactly as if it were an adjective. I have accordingly translated 'from this deathful body,' adopting the word 'deathful' as being analogous to 'sinful,' 'wrathful,' 'healthful,' &c. Perhaps 'mortal' would be better. For a decisive instance of this construction in the Septuagint I may refer to Prov. ix. 17, in which ὕδατος κλοπῆς γλυκεροῦ is 'sweet water of theft,' or 'sweet stolen water,' γλυκεροῦ necessarily agreeing with ὕδατος.

CHAPTER VIII. 1. The words μὴ κατὰ σάρκα κ.τ.λ., which conclude this verse in the received text, are insufficiently supported by MSS. They are not in Cod. Sin.

2. Some of the older MSS. with Cod. Sin. have σε in place of με. If this be the true reading—and unless it be it can hardly be accounted for—the singular of the second personal pronoun is here used, as the singular of the first personal pronoun was supposed to be used in the preceding Chapter, to designate *any* individual.

3. Περὶ ἁμαρτίας 'with reference to sin,' meaning that the sin of men was in a *prospective* manner taken account of by God in sending His Son into the world.

4. Τὸ δικαίωμα may differ from ἡ δικαιοσύνη only in being a more abstract noun, and probably it corresponds more closely than the latter to our word 'righteousness.'

5—7. 'Mind' in English is not only equivalent to ἡ φρὴν the intellectual faculty, but is also used both as a noun and as a verb in a moral sense, as in such phrases as "to have a mind to do a thing," "to mind one's business," &c. I have not been able to discover any more exact mode of expressing the senses of τὸ φρόνημα and φρονέω in this passage than that furnished by this usage of 'mind.'

8. The particle δὲ at the beginning of this verse appears neither to be adversative nor to be a copula. I consider it to be translated by putting a full stop at the end of verse 7.

9. The indefinite τις is perhaps better translated 'any one' than 'any man,' and οὗτος is more strictly 'this man' than 'he.' The "Five Clergymen" have not judged so.

11. Respecting the translation of ἐκ νεκρῶν by 'after death,' or 'from death,' see the Notes on vi. 11 and 13. The sentence, "will make alive also your mortal bodies," certainly seems to accord well with this rendering of ἐκ νεκρῶν.—The reading of the received text, διὰ τοῦ ἐνοικοῦντος κ.τ.λ., is in Cod. Sin.; but the authority of MSS. is on the whole in favour of διὰ with the accusative, which also gives a more appropriate sense than διὰ with the genitive. See Alford *in loco*.

12. I have exactly followed in the translation the order of the words in the original, this order appearing to be significant. The prominent position of ὀφειλέται may have been intended to make his word emphatic, and to convey the meaning, 'debtors we certainly are not to the flesh with respect to living according to flesh,' that is 'we owe nothing to flesh on that account.'

13. In this verse a reason is given why those who live according to flesh are not indebted to the flesh, viz. that they receive no profit therefrom, but the contrary, inasmuch as "they are ready to die." [For an instance like the adopted translation of μέλλετε ἀποθνήσκειν see Rev. iii. 2 in A. V.] This

reason, therefore, accords with the language held in vi. 21—23, "What fruit had ye then, &c.," and "The wages of sin is death." Alford is, I think, quite wrong in taking "we are debtors" to mean "we owe fealty."

15. In pagan writers ἡ δουλεία is 'bondage,' 'slavery,' that is, service in an unfavorable sense. But we have seen that St Paul speaks of two kinds of service, of serving "in the newness of spirit" as well as "in the oldness of letter" (vii. 6), and the same word δουλεύω applies to both services. In the present passage δουλεία is the service "in newness of spirit," and, therefore, cannot properly be called 'bondage.' The doctrine appears to be, that the new spirit of service which the saints receive does not again lead, as the former spirit did, to fear.

17. The occurrence of 'suffer' in this passage seems to have suggested to the apostle the statement of the doctrine that follows respecting suffering and hope and their mutual relation. It seemed to me that this doctrine should occupy a separate paragraph.

20. It is evident that ὑπετάγη cannot be taken in the passive signification 'was made subject,' because 'not of its own accord' follows, this being a superfluous assertion respecting that which is *made* subject. Hence the verb should be taken in the middle signification 'was' or 'became subject,' which it admits of notwithstanding its passive form. So the noun ἡ ὑποταγή is either subjecting one's self, i.e. obedience to any one, or subjection in consequence of being made subject.—As ἐλπίς is 'expectation' whether or not accompanied by hope, ἐπ' ἐλπίδι might here be translated 'in expectation,' in the sense of *anticipating* by a present act a future result, without reference to any uncertainty as to whether the result will take place. In this sense ἐπ' ἐλπίδι is used in 1 Cor. ix. 10 with respect to the husbandman who ploughs and sows in anticipation of harvest, the application of the metaphor turning upon the *certainty* of the ground of his expectation. For this reason I have ventured to translate the formula here 'in anticipation.'

24. The translation of Τῇ γὰρ ἐλπίδι ἐσώθημεν, 'For we are saved by hope,' as given in A. V., needs, I think, no alteration, the principle on which an aorist may be translated by a present being applicable to this passage. Hope is the more remote, faith the more immediate, means of salvation; although they are necessarily connected. The former agency is here expressed by a simple dative (τῇ ἐλπίδι), while the other is expressed (Eph. ii. 8) by διά with a genitive.—The word βλεπομένη shews that ἐλπίς is to be taken not as 'hope' abstractedly, but in the concrete signification of 'a hope.' Also 'seeing' may here be supposed to represent other senses, so that the argument is, a hope within sight, or within reach, is not properly a hope, it being attainable. Hoping for what is out of sight and reach implies patient waiting, and it is by this means that hope saves.

26. Ὡσαύτως 'in the same' or 'like manner' refers back to the agency of the Spirit described in verses 15 and 16. The Apostle now speaks of another operation of the Spirit, that of helping us in our weakness and ignorance with respect to prayer. This subject is, consequently, made to occupy a separate paragraph.—Τὸ τί 'what,' just as in Luke i. 62 and xix. 48.

—Καθὸ δεῖ might be translated 'becomingly.'—Whether or not we omit ὑπὲρ ἡμῶν, which is not found in some MSS., 'in our behalf' may be expressed, as being implied in ὑπερεντυγχάνει.—ἀλαλήτοις, 'that do not admit of being spoken.' The word 'uttered' is perhaps less exact than 'spoken.'

28. The particle δέ at the beginning of this verse is simply transitional, and as the transition is to a new subject, the verse begins a fresh paragraph. —κατὰ πρόθεσιν is literally 'according to purpose.' It cannot be more necessary to say in English than in Greek 'according to his purpose.' The word πρόθεσις is, however, generally used with respect to a purpose formed by the Creator from the beginning of the ages, and it is the occurrence of this word here that leads to what follows in verses 29 and 30 respecting divine foreknowledge and predestination.

29. The σὺν in συμμόρφους signifies the partaking of the saints *in common* of the image of God's Son, to the end that he might be "the firstborn among *many* brethren." The genitive τῆς εἰκόνος is dependent on συμμόρφους as if it were a substantive. Also the image, or likeness, of the Son of God is that form in which he was externally manifested to the world.

30. The aorists are used in this passage in such manner as to prove that they apply to future as well as past events; for the complete justification and glorification of the saints are certainly future.

31. Πρὸς ταῦτα may generally be rendered 'under these circumstances.' The adopted translation, 'these things being so,' gives a less formal turn to the expression, and at the same time accords with the phrase, "Are these things so?" occurring in the translation according to A. V. of Acts vii. 1, and also with the Latin *quæ cum ita sint*. The rendering, 'what shall we say to these things?' countenanced by the "Five Clergymen," is inexact.

39. οὔτε τις κτίσις ἑτέρα should, I think, be translated 'nor any other *creation*,' because the word κτίσις seems intended to comprehend the things present, things to come, powers, height, and depth, just before spoken of, which may be regarded as the essential constituents of the external creation of our experience. We find, in fact, that it is characterized by relations of *time* and *space*, and by the agency of *natural powers* in time and space; and apparently we may infer from the Apostle's reference to these principles that he intends to say that neither a creation constituted like the present one, nor any other, will be able to separate us from the love of God.

CHAPTER IX. 1. That μοι is governed by σὺν in συμμαρτυρούσης may be inferred from the following consideration. The Apostle asserts that he speaks the truth "in Christ," speaking being an *outward* act; and he adds that his conscience bears witness in the Holy Spirit *with him thus speaking*, because the operation of conscience is *inward*. Alford says, inaccurately, that "joint testimony" is not signified.

3. The imperfect indicative ηὐχόμην has no other meaning than 'I desired' or 'I was desiring,' and is correctly rendered 'optabam' by Jerome. The expression 'I could wish' means 'I am disposed to wish, and might wish, did not some strong reason prevent,' that is, actually, I do not wish; which, certainly, is not what ηὐχόμην is capable of expressing. Rather, the Apostle is here stating, as the cause of his "great sorrow and continual

anguish" that at one time he desired to be "accursed from Christ." This expression exhibits the deep sense he now has of the state of mind he was in when, as he says, he was "a blasphemer, a persecutor, and injurious" (1 Tim. i. 13). That his former persecution of the Church of Christ was a source of continual sorrow to him,—of that godly sorrow that works repentance,—is evident from the number of times he refers to it in his Epistles, and the language in which he speaks of it. See 1 Cor. xv. 9, Gal. i. 13 and 14, Phil. iii. 6, 1 Tim. i. 13, and Acts xxvi. 9.

This interpretation, however, requires that αὐτὸς ἐγώ should precede ἀνάθεμα εἶναι, as is the case in the textus receptus, and Scholz's edition, and this reading is supported by MSS. of good authority. But the majority of the ancient MSS., and among them the Cod. Sinait., have αὐτὸς ἐγώ after ἀνάθεμα εἶναι. The transposition may, possibly, have been made from misunderstanding the passage, and comparing it with Exodus xxxii. 32.

6. In the three preceding verses the Apostle states that at one time he himself acted as one who desired to be accursed from Christ, and intimates that he did so out of zeal for the Jewish religion, perceiving that the doctrine of Christ was contrary to the special privileges of the Jews. By saying emphatically αὐτὸς ἐγώ he implies that he did then what his unbelieving countrymen were still doing, and from the same motive. The early persecutions of Christians by the Jews all had reference to the doctrine of the extension of salvation to the Gentiles. In the present passage St Paul argues that although the privileges of the Jews do not, as such, secure their salvation, as is evident from their opposition to Christ, yet the word and the will of God have not on that account failed of effect, inasmuch as not all that are of Israel are Israel, but those only who become children of God by faith. The adopted translation of οὐχ οἷον δὲ ὅτι, 'not so, however, as that,' accords with this interpretation, the particle δὲ having here the sense of 'however.' In English we may say 'as that,' analogously to saying 'as if,' or 'as though.'

9. The strict rendering of κατὰ τὸν καιρὸν τοῦτον is, 'according to this season,' meaning the season of the year; not simply 'at this time,' as given in A.V. The Septuagint has κατὰ τὸν καιρὸν τοῦτον εἰς ὥρας.

10. Here, as in a great number of like instances, the verb substantive is omitted. In this ellipsis the object is abstractedly regarded as being in view. Our idiom requires the indication 'there is' to be expressed.

11. 'Might remain' is adopted as being a stricter translation of μένῃ than 'might stand.'

15—18. The usual punctuation of v. 15 is erroneous, the construction being taken as if ὃν ἂν in the first clause were governed by ἐλεήσω and in the other by οἰκτειρήσω, whereas the governing verbs are respectively ἐλεῶ and οἰκτείρω, and commas should be put after ἐλεήσω and οἰκτειρήσω. I have translated accordingly. This correction has an important bearing on the Apostle's doctrine. The assertion *here* is not, as in *v.* 18, that God will have mercy on whom he chooses to have mercy, but simply that he will have mercy, whoever may be the recipients of his mercy, as is signified by the indefinite pronoun ὃν ἂν, *quemcunque*. To point out this sense of the words is the particular purpose of the Apostle's remark, "Therefore it is not of one that wills, neither of one that runs, but of God shewing mercy." [The clause, "nor of one that runs," only serves to give distinctness to the more abstract expression "one that wills," running being an outward and visible act of the will]. In short, in the passage from Exodus God declares to Moses his purpose of being merciful. But the mercy of the Creator and Ruler of all things necessitates that his power and anger be also manifested, because mercy to some implies danger to all. There must, consequently, be difference of dealing towards different individuals to give room for the manifestation of mercy; and this difference is not of mere arbitrary will, but of will acting in subordination to the purpose of shewing mercy. For these reasons the Apostle concludes the argument by saying (in v. 18), "*Therefore* he has mercy on whom it is his will to have mercy, and whom it is his will to harden he hardens." In the Authorized Version the form of expression in v. 15 is not distinguished from the different form (ὃν θέλει ἐλεεῖ) in v. 18, and consequently the argument is not exhibited.

20. The particle, or rather combination of particles, μενοῦνγε, occurs in three other places in the New Testament, Rom. x. 18, Luke xi. 28, and Phil. iii. 8. We may not unreasonably presume that this peculiar word has the same meaning in all the instances. On trial I think it will be found that 'in deed' suits each passage, not, however, in the sense in which the simple conjunction μέν is sometimes rendered 'indeed,' but more emphatically in the sense of 'in truth,' 'in reality.'

20—23. The answer given in this passage to the questions, "Why does He yet find fault? Who resists His will?" indicates that the scheme of God's manifestation of His power, with respect both to the "vessels of wrath" and the "vessels of mercy," is formative, or *creative*, in its character; being, in fact, as a whole, what I have previously called "a spiritual creation," comprehending at once the hardness of heart of the vessels of wrath "fitted for destruction," and the preparation for future glory of those who are chosen to be vessels of mercy. Also it seems that these two aspects of the spiritual creation are related to each other, the former being antecedent and introductory to the other, as in the natural creation the reign of darkness and disorder preceded the creation of light and life. Such relation is expressly indicated in verses 22 and 23, if only they be correctly interpreted. No philological reason can be given for the translation 'but what if' of εἰ δὲ at the beginning of v. 22, which, probably, was thought of only because it was not noticed that καὶ at the beginning of v. 23 indicates the beginning of the apodosis of the sentence. This is a mistake of the same kind as that which, as I have already pointed out, led to ascribing to St Paul an unreasonably long parenthetical sentence in Rom. v. The apodosis filled up would be, 'also [he endured in much longsuffering vessels of wrath fitted for destruction] in order that he might make known &c.' In English we may substitute for the words in brackets 'it was,' and omit rendering καί; but in the idiom of the Greek of the New Testament this expression would not be adopted, because it involves the use of the verb εἰμί, but instead of it the beginning of the apodosis might be indicated by καί.

From this doctrine of the Apostle we may, as it seems, conclude that vessels of wrath, created for the manifestation of God's power and anger in subservience to the creation of vessels of mercy, are fitted for destruction because wrath does not require to be for ever manifested, being eventually succeeded by mercy, when the spiritual creation is complete, and all have become recipients of mercy. For God is a "faithful Creator" and "there is no unrighteousness in Him."

27. The δέ at the beginning of this verse seems to be in some degree adversative. A comparison of the number of the sons of Israel with the sand of the sea occurs in Hosea i. 6, in connection with the passage quoted in v. 25 from that prophet; but in Isaiah it is asserted that although the sons of Israel be thus numerous, that which remains (τὸ κατάλειμμα) shall be saved, and the reason is added, that God is finishing his work and will complete it in righteousness. It is particularly to be noticed that the abstract noun, τὸ κατάλειμμα, signifies that which results from God's perfect work, namely, as the context shews, a countless number of sons of Israel in a state of salvation. With this agrees the vision of the Apostle John, in which he saw "a great multitude whom no man could number," clothed in white robes, and heard them ascribe their salvation to God and the Lamb (Rev. vii. 9, 10). This company is distinct from that spoken of in Rev. vii. 3—8, which consists of a *limited* number of *sealed* servants of God, *elected* out of the twelve tribes of Israel. The latter is the company of the *elect*. But to understand this doctrine it must be borne in mind that "Israel," "sons of Israel," and "twelve tribes of Israel," are terms ever increasing in comprehension as the great work of God advances towards completion.

28. I translate λόγον 'work,' as in A. V., rather than 'word' for the sake of the English reader. In the Apostle's time, as well as when Isaiah wrote, it may have been generally understood that with respect to creation, the word and the work of God are the same thing. "He spake and it was done." In 2 Esdras vi. 38 we read, "Thy word was a perfect work." The verbs συντελῶ and συντέμνω have here, as in other instances adduced by Schleusner, nearly the same meaning. The "Five Clergymen," by translating λόγον 'reckoning,' and λόγον συντετμημένον 'a short reckoning,' have altogether missed the sense of the passage.

29. The meaning seems to be, 'We should have been as Sodom' in respect to its *destruction*, and in the same respect 'we should have resembled Gomorrah.' I have, therefore, rendered the ὡς before Gomorrah in the same manner as that before Sodom. The English language does not reject the combination 'like as.'

30. By translating κατέλαβε 'took hold of' in accordance with the proper meaning of the verb, the contrast with οὐκ ἔφθασε, 'did not attain to,' in v. 31 is better exhibited than by the translations 'attained to' and 'arrived not at' adopted in R. A. V.

31. The textus receptus has δικαιοσύνης after the second νόμον, but in the Cod. Sin., and the older MSS. generally, this word is omitted. Whether or not it be retained, the second νόμον must, I think, receive the same interpretation as the first; that is, it signifies the moral law regarded as the rule of righteousness to them who believe. Compare x. 2—11, the doctrine in which passage appears to consist of an amplification of that in the present one.

32. 'It was' is here supplied on the principle indicated in the remarks on v. 23.

CHAPTER X. 1. As εἰς σωτηρίαν may be taken to express the end to which the heart's desire and prayer of the Apostle were directed, and not any actual effect, it may be translated 'for' or 'towards their salvation,' the preposition εἰς with the accusative admitting of this meaning.

2. Μαρτυρῶ αὐτοῖς, 'I testify to them,' 'I bear witness to them,' not concerning them. The Apostle assures them by his testimony that they have a zeal of, or from, God, that is, according to godliness, but not according to knowledge. How many in all ages need to be told that they have religious zeal unaccompanied by knowledge!

3. Στῆσαι, 'to establish.' See iii. 31. The "Five Clergymen" translate τῇ δικαιοσύνῃ in this verse and εἰς δικαιοσύνην in the next, 'unto righteousness.' Surely a distinction should be made. For the sake of distinction I have generally translated εἰς with the accusative 'unto,' and in no case have I taken 'unto' to be equivalent to 'to,' as it often appears to be in A. V. Thus without ambiguity τῇ δικαιοσύνῃ is 'to the righteousness.'

5. The double accusative after γράφω both expresses what is written, and indicates also the subject of the writing. (See Liddell and Scott *sub voc.*) The ὅτι which introduces the quotation (Lev. xviii. 5) is sufficiently taken into account by the punctuation, and by beginning the quotation with a capital letter. The aorist participle ποιήσας is here correctly translated in A.V. as if it were a present, on a principle relative to the aorist which has already been several times adverted to. See on v. 12.

9. Ὅτι is rightly translated 'that' in A.V., because it signifies that what follows is "the word of faith" just before spoken of.

11. The literal rendering is, 'Every one that believes on him shall not be ashamed,' that is, shall be exempt from shame. The adopted translation is more conformable to English idiom.

12. In the negative assertion, 'there is no difference,' ἐστί is expressed; but in the ideally positive assertion, 'there is the same Lord of all,' the substantive verb is, as usual, omitted. See iii. 29 and 30.

13. 'Whosoever' may be considered to translate sufficiently πᾶς ὃς ἄν.

17. This parenthetical remark was occasioned by the occurrence of ἀκοή in the quotation from Isaiah in the sense of 'report,' that is, something proclaimed, the same word having also the simple signification of 'hearing.' Since what is believed is something heard, 'belief from report' and 'belief from hearing' are facts so necessarily related, that in Greek one is expressed in the very same terms as the other.

18. Respecting the translation μενοῦνγε see the remarks on ix. 20. Τὰ πέρατα, 'bounds,' 'limits,' rather than 'ends.'

19. Πρῶτος seems here to be used in a manner analogous to the use of πρῶτον in iii. 2. See the remarks on that passage. By consulting Deut. xxxii. 21 it will be seen that the jealousy or anger of Israel is not said to be excited 'against' any nation, but that God is said to employ a nation that is no nation, or a foolish nation, to provoke them to jealousy or anger, as they had provoked him "with their vanities."

20. Πρός is here 'towards' rather than 'unto.'

CHAPTER XI. 1. The question here asked is equivalent to this: Is an Israelite, as being an Israelite, cast off by God? The Apostle answers that it is not so, inasmuch as he is himself an Israelite; the force of which reason depends upon his having been chosen to be an "apostle of Christ," and the consequent certainty of his not being one whom God has cast off. This leads him to point out the distinction between Israel according to the flesh and the elect Israel whom God foreknew.

2. The strict translation, 'what the Scripture says *in* Elijah,' is intelligible enough if we consider that the sayings and doings of chosen servants of God, like Elijah, constitute in great part what the Scripture speaks.

4. I have already adopted, after A. V., the word 'oracle' for translating τὰ λόγια in iii. 2. There seems, however, to be better reason for using it to translate ὁ χρηματισμός, this being the proper Greek word for an oracular response. It requires, however, to be qualified by 'divine' or 'of God,' because χρηματισμὸς commonly signifies a pagan oracle.

5. It might seem, at first view, that ἐν τῷ νῦν καιρῷ refers to the particular epoch at which the Apostle was writing. But in that case the reason for the inferential οὖν does not clearly appear, nor is it evident why the expression should be preceded by καὶ in the sense of 'even.' I rather take ἐν τῷ νῦν καιρῷ to mean 'in the present age of the world,' and the assertion of St Paul to be that at any time, even in the present age, a certain number of God's elect remain living after the departure of those who lived before them. To signify this it seems that λεῖμμα is used rather than κατάλειμμα, the latter word embracing the whole of the elect, who remain assembled together in the resurrection state, after the present age has come to an end, and the number of the elect is completed.

6. The doctrine of salvation by grace is thrown in here parenthetically with reference to the applicability of the terms, "according to the election of grace," to the "remnant" just before spoken of.

8. The course of the sentence is interrupted by the passage between dashes, in order to give immediate support to the word 'blinded' by a citation from the Scriptures, in accordance with a principle of reasoning on points of doctrine which is frequently employed by St Paul.

10. Τοῦ μὴ βλέπειν, 'to the effect that they see not,' more strictly, perhaps, than 'in order that they may not see.'

13 and 14. These verses are put in brackets, because the Apostle here suspends the argument for the purpose of signifying to those whom he is writing to that he is now speaking more especially to the Gentiles, and that he does so in order to give prominence to his office of apostle to the Gentiles, that by thus exciting to jealousy his countrymen he may save some of them. In MSS. A B and the Cod. Sin., and in Lachmann's edition, the reading after ὑμῖν is δὲ instead of γάρ. I have adopted this reading, and consider it to be taken account of by the punctuation and the brackets.

15. The argument is resumed at the beginning of this verse to the following effect: If the rejection of Israel according to the flesh be the reconciling of the world, what can reception into favour be, if not life after death? It is to be noticed that ἡ πρόσληψις is to be taken in an abstract sense, without limitation of the recipients of favour to the people of the

Jews, the pronoun αὐτῶν not being repeated. In fact the terms, "life after death," which describe the favour, shew that the whole Israel of God, consisting both of Jews and Gentiles, partake of it in the resurrection state of the age to come. [I have already given reasons for translating ἐκ νεκρῶν 'after death.']

16. St James says (i. 18) that they who are begotten by the word of truth, i.e. the faithful, are "a kind of firstfruits of God's creations" (κτισμάτων); and from Rev. xiv. 1—4, we learn that the chosen number who are "redeemed from among men" are "the firstfruits to God and the Lamb." The same idea is plainly in the mind of St Paul, inasmuch as he goes on to say (v. 16), "if the firstfruit be holy, the lump is holy ; and if the root be holy, the branches are holy." Here "firstfruit" represents God's elect, and the "lump" the innumerable company of the saved spoken of in Rev. vii. 9. So also "the root" means the foreknown Israel, and "the branches" represent the rest of the world, whether Jew or Gentile, regarded as being related to this root.

17. After thus briefly adverting, by the way, to the more remote consequences of his doctrine the Apostle proceeds (in v. 17 and the following verses to the end of the Chapter) to speak of the mutual relation of Jew and Gentile, *in the present age*, with respect to the scheme of salvation actually in progress, using for the purpose the emblems of a wild olive, and of a good olive with its branches and root. According to this exegesis the translation of v. 17 should begin, 'Now if some, &c.'

18. The "Five Clergymen" translate, 'it is not thou that bearest the root, but the root thee,' whereas the Greek expresses 'it is not that thou bearest the root, but the root thee.'

21. Μήπως is not in MSS. ABC, nor in Cod. Sin., and is omitted by Lachmann. The omission seems to be required by the future indicative φείσεται, which reading is found in most of the ancient MSS.

22. I adopt, with Alford, the readings ἀποτομία and χρηστότης θεοῦ, which are given in Cod. Sin., as well as in other ancient MSS. In the next clause τῇ χρηστότητι does not appear to mean the goodness, i.e. benevolence of God, but the goodness which a believer partakes of by the grace of God, according to which interpretation this word stands opposed to τῇ ἀπιστίᾳ in the next verse. Apparently for the purpose of distinguishing between the two senses in which the same word is used, the first χρηστότης is followed by θεοῦ, which adjunct is, however, omitted in many MSS., probably because, through misunderstanding of the passage, it was thought to be tautological.

23. I have translated κἀκεῖνοι δὲ simply 'and they,' considering δὲ to be taken into account by the punctuation. I do not see how the exact rendering can be 'and they also,' as in A.V., much less how it can be 'yea and they,' as proposed by the "Five Clergymen."

24. The translation 'from the olive-tree which is by nature wild,' adopted by the "Five Clergymen," might lead the English reader to suppose that St Paul is here referring to a general characteristic of the olive-tree, whereas he is speaking of a known kind of olive-tree naturally wild. The Vulgate has, ex naturali oleastro, distinguishing thus the wild olive (oleaster)

from the good olive (oliva). The ambiguity will be avoided by taking the article τῆς to be equivalent to the English indefinite article 'an,' and translating 'from an olive wild by nature.' (See on this philological point what is said in the Introduction.)

25—27. The subject-matter of these verses is parenthetical with respect to the context, but yet requires to be understood in order that the Apostle's reasoning may be fully appreciated. For understanding it we must first ascertain who are called "Israel" in verse 25, and who are "all Israel" in v. 26. The first question is answered by the Apostle himself by his saying, "I would not that ye should be ignorant, brethren, of this mystery, lest ye be wise in your own conceits, that blindness in part has befallen Israel, &c." The caution as to being "wise in their own conceits" cannot possibly have any application unless the "brethren" addressed in this Epistle, who at the beginning of it are said to be "called saints" and "beloved of God," are included in the "Israel" on whom blindness in part has fallen. The caution was needed lest they who have the evidence in themselves that they are "the called of Jesus Christ," should suppose that they are perfect in knowledge and in the graces accompanying knowledge. For St Paul asserts (1 Cor. xiii. 12), identifying himself with believers in general, "Now I know in part; then I shall know as also I am known." And again (in v. 10 of the same Chapter), "when that which is perfect is come, then that which is in part shall be done away."

The second question admits of being answered as follows. In the passage to which this enquiry relates, the time at which the existing state of partial blindness of the true Israel begins to cease, is spoken of as the time when "the completion of the nations has come in," that is, when the series of the successive empires and kingdoms of the present world is completed, and the end of the age has arrived. This is the epoch of "the resurrection of the just," at which the elect saints of all ages and all nations will be gathered together. This assembly constitutes the people which is here called "all Israel."

But this people has not yet been made perfect. Therefore "The Deliverer" (who, doubtless, is Jesus Christ, performing at his second appearing the part of righteous Judge) "comes to Sion," and sets out "from Sion," "to turn away ungodliness from Jacob," that is, from God's elect, and to make with them "a new covenant" in virtue of which their sins will be entirely and for ever done away. But this œconomy is not completed in a day, nor in a few days. The transactions of that "age" are very largely spoken of by the prophets of the Old Testament; and generally it is this period which is referred to wherever they say "in that day." The passage quoted by St Paul from Isaiah (lix. 20) is one among many which speak of the dispensation by which the saints are hereafter made perfect. In the New Testament the same proceedings seem to be indicated where it is said of the apostles of the Lord that "they shall sit on twelve thrones judging the twelve tribes of Israel."

This doctrine respecting the imperfection of the elect in the present age, and the transactions in which they will be concerned in the age to come, is called by the Apostle "a mystery," which, however he was unwilling that the faithful of his time should be "ignorant of." If any Christians were ignorant of it then, much more is this the case now; for in these days scarcely any one appears to give attention to what Scripture reveals respecting the events which must come to pass in the age of the world that follows upon the present one.

The bearing of the passage within brackets on the general argument of the Apostle may perhaps be seen from the foregoing remarks, and from what was previously said on verses 15 and 16.

29. Ἀμεταμέλητα, 'without repentance,' may be taken in nearly the same sense as 'with whom is no variableness' in Jam. i. 17.

31. The tenor of the argument absolutely requires that τῷ ὑμετέρῳ ἐλέει should be joined with the clause preceding, and not as in A. V. and the Revision by "Five Clergymen," with the clause following. The mercy shewn to Gentiles in a state of unbelief gave occasion to unbelief on the part of the Jews, so that all, both Jews and Gentiles, have been included in unbelief, that God might have mercy on all. This argument implies that a state of unbelief and impenitence precedes, as it were *by a general law*, the bestowal and reception of God's favour. The same truth may, in fact, be gathered from the doctrine expressed in *v.* 32.

32. Συνέκλεισε, 'has shut up together.' This translation, for conformity with English idiom, of the aorist by a perfect past, necessitates translating ἵνα ἐλεήσῃ 'that he *may* have mercy.' The strict translation 'that he *might* have mercy' applies only in case συνέκλεισε be rendered as an aorist.

33. Considering that St Paul frequently uses the word πλοῦτος in the general sense of 'abundance,' I adhere to the translation in A. V. of the first clause of this verse. The original of the second clause may be exactly represented by translating ἀνεξιχνίαστοι, as well as ἀνεξερεύνητα, by a single English word. The former is strictly 'untraceable,' and this sense is applicable here; but in Eph. iii. 8 the same word may be appropriately rendered 'unsearchable.'

34 and 35. The aorists are rendered as perfect past tenses for the same reason as in *v.* 32. In *v.* 35 the second αὐτῷ refers to τίς in the first clause. This is expressed by the adopted translation.

CHAPTER XII. 1. Λογικήν, 'reasonable,' as in A.V., the service being such that good reasons can be given for it. See 1 Pet. iii. 15, where λόγος is used with respect to giving a reason.

2. I have translated μὴ συσχηματίζεσθαι in accordance with the A. V. rendering of συσχηματιζόμενοι ταῖς ἐπιθυμίαις in 1 Pet. i. 14, and with that of τὸ σχῆμα τοῦ κόσμου τούτου in 1 Cor. vii. 31.

The epithets 'good,' 'acceptable,' 'perfect' cannot belong to 'will' (τὸ θέλημα), because will is something *sui generis*, the character of which we perceive by personal experience, but which does not admit of degree or qualification. What is called 'free will' is liberty to act according to one's wish; "a strong will" means the display of much *power* in acting according to one's wish. But every *personal act* is an act of the will, whether or not it be according to our inclination, and although it may be determined by attendant circumstances, which are partly, or wholly, beyond our control. The act of a criminal in walking to the place of execution is an act of his will, determined by what he judges to be best under the circumstances in which he is placed. Now since God is omnipotent, and can fulfil His own pleasure, and since that which is good, and acceptable, and perfect accords with His pleasure, it follows that what is so characterized may be put in apposition with "the will of God." I have translated accordingly.

3. An endeavour has been made to express in English all that is signified by the repetition of φρονεῖν in the original.

6—8. The grammatical construction of this passage, which the terminal indications of the cases render sufficiently clear in the original, is with difficulty exhibited in a translation into English. That ἔχοντες χαρίσματα at the beginning of v. 6 depends on 'we' the understood nominative of ἐσμεν, 'we are,' in v. 5, is readily seen. In order to shew that the accusatives προφητείαν in v. 6 and διακονίαν in v. 7 are in apposition with χαρίσματα, I translate 'gift of prophecy,' 'gift of ministration.' The passage included within dashes, which interrupts the regular course of the construction, seems to have been thrown in for the purpose of distinguishing between two classes of gifts,—those relating to prophecy or teaching, and those relating to ministration or active duty,—before proceeding to shew how the many who constitute one body in Christ are severally members one of another. The construction is taken up in v. 7 by εἴτε ὁ διδάσκων, this nominative being in apposition with 'we' the nominative of ἐσμεν. The same is the case with the succeeding nominatives ὁ παρακαλῶν, ὁ μεταδιδούς, ὁ προϊστάμενος, ὁ ἐλεῶν; while the adjuncts ἐν τῇ διακονίᾳ, ἐν τῇ διδασκαλίᾳ, ἐν τῇ παρακλήσει, ἐν ἁπλότητι, ἐν σπουδῇ, and ἐν ἱλαρότητι, respectively point out by what offices, or by what graces, the several members of the body become members one of another.—I interpret ἐν ἁπλότητι in accordance with our Lord's teaching in Matth. vi. 1—4 and in Luke vi. 30—36, inferring from these passages that 'to give in simplicity' is to give without shew, or boasting, or respect of persons, or hope of return, but simply because it is Godlike so to do, and does good to the recipient. This, in fact, is true liberality.

9. At the beginning of this verse there is a change of construction which might be supposed to indicate that the Apostle's language here becomes hortatory; in which case the translation would be, 'Let love be without hypocrisy,' ἔστω being understood. As however this ellipsis is unusual, I have preferred taking the sentences in verses 9—13 as *descriptive* of various Christian graces and practices. Such teaching, however, is so closely connected with exhortation, that they are nearly equivalent, and one naturally runs into the other. Of this we have had an instance in vi. 19. In the passage before us, after the commencement at v. 14 of express exhortation, 'Bless them, &c.,' the following verses to the end of the Chapter contain several alternations between descriptive teaching and direct exhortation.

I have rendered ἡ ἀγάπη ἀνυπόκριτος, '*our* love without hypocrisy,' not because I admit that the Greek article is ever equivalent to a pronoun, but because this rendering shews that ἀποστυγοῦντες (v. 9), translated 'haters,' is in the *first* person, agreeing with 'we' in v. 5, and by this means the construction of the Greek is indicated.

10. The translation of φιλαδελφίᾳ adopted by the "Five Clergymen" is 'love of the brethren.' That it should rather be 'brotherly love' may, I think, be inferred from the use of this word in other passages, particularly 1 Pet. iii. 8 and 2 Pet. i. 7. Alford translates φιλάδελφοι in the former of these passages, 'loving the brethren,' and φιλαδελφία in the latter, 'brotherly kindness.' In A. V. the renderings are consistent.—Τῇ τιμῇ ἀλλήλους προηγούμενοι may well be compared with ἀλλήλους ἡγούμενοι ὑπερέχοντας ἑαυτῶν in Phil. ii. 3. As ἡγούμενοι in the latter passage means 'esteeming,' it would be no stretch of philological principle to take προηγούμενοι to mean 'esteeming in preference,' even though there should not be independent authority for this sense of the word. It does not appear that in any other way an appropriate meaning can be extracted from the Greek. The translation of the "Five Clergymen," 'in giving honour outdoing one another,' seems hardly consistent with other Scriptural teaching.

11. Σπουδή is primarily 'diligence, or earnestness, in the performance of a task or duty.' Here it seems to be put for the duty which requires to be so done. 'Studium' in Latin, and 'study' in English, have analogous double senses.

13. Κοινωνοῦντες governing a dative, 'sharing in,' 'participating in ;' that is, communicating to saints in their necessities, and not, as proposed by the "Five Clergymen," 'communicating to their necessities.'

16. Συναπαγόμενοι, literally 'led away along with.' I have not been able to discover any rendering which seems more appropriate than 'acquiescing in.' The marginal translation of A. V., 'be contented with mean things,' approaches closely to that I have adopted.

18. This verse is usually wrongly punctuated. There should be no comma in A.V. after 'If it be possible ;' for evidently if 'as far as depends on you' (τὸ ἐξ ὑμῶν) be joined with what follows, 'if it be possible' is superfluous. The meaning is, 'If, so far as depends on you, it be possible, be at peace, &c.'

19. Δότε τόπον τῇ ὀργῇ, 'give place to anger,' that is, the anger of the "enemy" mentioned in v. 20. With this precept may be compared μὴ ἀποδιδόντες λοιδορίαν ἀντί λοιδορίας, "not returning railing for railing," in 1 Pet. iii. 9, also, "a soft answer turns away wrath" (Prov. xv. 1). The word in the Septuagint corresponding to 'soft' is ὑποπίπτουσα, 'submissive,' 'yielding.'

CHAPTER XIII. 2. The articles in τῇ ἐξουσίᾳ and τῇ διαταγῇ, as in many other instances, simply individualize, being equivalent to the indefinite article 'a.'—Ἑαυτοῖς κρίμα λήψονται is literally 'will take to themselves,' or 'receive for themselves judgment.' In English we say 'will bring on themselves judgment,' the metaphor only being changed. I have translated accordingly. The context shews that κρίμα is here judgment necessarily involving penal consequence; but it is not the same thing as "condemnation" after trial, which is κατάκριμα.

3. The reading τῷ ἀγαθῷ ἔργῳ, ἀλλὰ τῷ κακῷ, which is given in the

majority of ancient MSS., being adopted, for the sake of consistency, οὐκ εἰσὶ φόβος is translated 'do not deter from.'—The clause beginning θέλεις δὲ may either be interrogative, or suppositional. The latter sense is, I think, preferable.

4. Since at the end of v. 3 we have, 'thou wilt have praise from it,' i.e. from the power, it seems proper to take the power, and not the person who exercises it, as the agency spoken of in the clauses following.

6. 'For on this account ye also pay tribute' is thrown in parenthetically, as coming under the category of the preceding doctrine, and at the same time indicating the sense in which 'for conscience' sake' is to be taken. The argument is resumed after the parenthesis by the sentence beginning λειτουργοὶ γὰρ θεοῦ εἰσιν, 'for there exist ministers of God.' The ministers here referred to appear to be angels: for we have in Heb. i. 7, "who makes his angels spirits, and his ministers (λειτουργοὺς) a flame of fire;" and again in Heb. i. 14, "Are not they (i.e. the angels) all ministering spirits (λειτουργικὰ πνεύματα) sent forth for service (διακονίαν) in behalf of them who shall be heirs of salvation?" Thus the offices of the heavenly angels, in respect to punishing the wicked and defending the good, are symbolized and represented by those of earthly potentates, as kings, magistrates, &c.; and it is for this reason that the latter are to be obeyed "for conscience' sake." This view accounts for the second γὰρ in v. 6, as well as for the assertion that these ministers of God "attend continually to this very thing" (αὐτὸ τοῦτο), that is, are, like the earthly powers, agents for awarding honour, or inflicting punishment.

7. The accusatives τὸν φόνον, τὸ τέλος, κ.τ.λ., may be referred to 'ye owe' understood, this being the correlative of ἀπόδοτε. Alford takes αἰτοῦντι to be the correlative of ἀπόδοτε; but this word could not well be supplied before τὸν φόβον, or τὴν τιμήν.—A new series of instructions, differing for the most part from those which precede, commence at v. 7, on which account this verse is put at the beginning of a paragraph.

8. Τὸν ἕτερον is correctly translated 'another' in A. V., regard being had to the usage of the article. The translation 'his neighbour' given in the R.A.V. does not represent the original.

9. Εἴ τις ἑτέρα ἐντολή, 'any other commandment that there is,' that is, 'every other commandment.' In Cod. Sin. ἐστὶν is supplied, the clause not expressing any doubt. Ἀνακεφαλαιοῦται is in the singular number on account of Τὸ at the beginning of the verse, which refers inclusively to all the commands that follow. Consequently the nominative 'it' is not required.

10. Τῷ πλησίον, 'to a neighbour,' the article pointing to any individual who may be near. If, with A.V. and R.A.V., we translate 'to his neighbour,' the pronoun 'his' will have no personal antecedent.

11. Εἰδότες, 'knowing.' This participle is shewn to be in the first person plural by rendering ἡμᾶς in the next clause.

13. I have thought it right to translate the clause ὡς ἐν ἡμέρᾳ in the order in which it occurs in the original, because this order seems to shew that "the day" here is not ordinary day-time, but that day which is spoken of in the preceding verse. According to this view, the translation 'as if in the day' will signify that the faithful ought to conduct themselves as if "the day"

which succeeds "the night" of the present age of the world had already come. See the remarks on vi. 11.

14. Generally πρόνοια signifies 'prudence,' 'forethought.' But πρόνοιαν ποιεῖσθε can hardly be, 'take forethought,' if the proper meaning of ποιεῖσθε be considered. It seems rather to be, 'put forethought in practice,' that is, 'make provision.' The preposition εἰς may serve to indicate the direction and purpose of the forethought; so that the complete sense of the clause appears to be, 'make not provision for the flesh for the purpose of fulfilling its lusts;' or more briefly, 'make not provision for the flesh out of regard to its lusts.' This doctrine implies that we are to abstain, not from all provision for the flesh, but from providing expressly for the gratification of fleshly lusts.

On re-consideration of this comment I felt much doubt as to whether the genitive τῆς σαρκὸς, taken as dependent on πρόνοιαν, can be thus interpreted. It would not be inconsistent with St Paul's style to make τῆς σαρκὸς dependent on ἐπιθυμίας and regard πρόνοιαν ποιεῖσθε as a verb. I have translated accordingly, although the above comment is allowed to stand.

CHAPTER XIV. 1. Διακρίσεις διαλογισμῶν, seems to be 'discussion, or sifting of doubtful thoughts' rather than 'decision of doubts,' nearly in agreement with 'judging of doubtful thoughts' in the marginal rendering of A. V.

4. Ἀλλότριον οἰκέτην, 'another's servant,' not 'the servant of another man,' because the context shews that his owner is the Lord. The reading ὁ κύριος at the end of the verse is better supported by MSS. than ὁ θεός. Hence as ὁ κύριος is 'the Lord,' it seems to follow that τῷ ἰδίῳ κυρίῳ must be 'to his own Lord.' This interpretation is confirmed by the positive assertion, σταθήσεται δέ, 'but he shall stand,' or 'be made to stand'; for this must be effected by that Lord who alone is able to make him stand.

6. The reading of the Cod. Sin. and the majority of the ancient MSS. is followed.

9. The weight of early authority is in favour of the reading ἀπέθανε καὶ ἔζησεν. It is not necessary to take ἔζησεν in the sense of 'lived again,' because the aorist expresses the objective fact that Christ lived, both with reference to his life in the present world, and to that in the world to come.

10. The Apostle distinguishes between him who judges, and him who despises, particularly by the formula, ἢ καὶ σύ, the strict rendering of which is, 'or also thou.'—The earlier MSS., with Cod. Sin., have τοῦ θεοῦ in place of τοῦ Χριστοῦ.

12. Ἄρα οὖν, 'therefore,' the combination of these particles being indicative of a formal conclusion.

13. We may say in English 'to judge a person,' and also 'to judge of a person or thing.' In the present passage the same verb κρίνω is used in both senses.—Τὸ μὴ τιθέναι, literally 'the not putting,' which is simply expressing the negative of a fact. But so far as personal will is concerned this expression must mean 'to avoid putting' or 'to abstain from putting.'

14. The full meaning of this passage is, nothing is unclean of itself; nothing is unclean except it be to him who accounts any thing to be unclean: to that man the thing is unclean. This sense appears to be conveyed

by translating εἰ μή 'only.' For distinguishing between τῷ and ἐκείνῳ I have translated the latter 'to that man.'

15. The 'for' refers to what is said in verse 13, verse 14 being parenthetical.

17. I doubt whether 'righteousness in the Holy Spirit' is a possible expression, because righteousness is essentially external, consisting in outward acts. But peace and joy are gifts of the Spirit, following upon the grace of righteousness. (See Rom. v. 1, 2.) The adopted punctuation connects only ' peace and joy ' with 'in the Holy Spirit.'

18. Ἐν τούτῳ, 'in this,' refers not to righteousness only, but to righteousness accompanied by peace and joy in the Holy Spirit. In fact, the brief description of "the kingdom of God" in verse 17 is an epitome of the life and experience of a Christian ; and it seems that for this reason the Apostle says 'in this' as if speaking of something well understood, and not requiring the addition of a substantive to define it.

20. The translation of κατάλυε by 'undo,' as proposed in R. A.V. well expresses the distinction between this verb and ἀπόλλυε in v. 15.

21. I translate τὸ μὴ φαγεῖν 'to abstain from eating' on the principle stated in the note to verse 13. According to this translation, μηδὲ ἐν ᾧ, the syntax of which it is otherwise difficult to account for, may be conveniently rendered, 'or any thing wherein.'

22. Σὺ πίστιν ἔχεις, 'thou hast faith,' the affirmative rendering being analogous to that already adopted for the clause beginning θέλεις δὲ in xiii. 3. —Δοκιμάζει, 'approves.' This probably is the meaning of ' alloweth' in A. V. The sense of the passage appears to be, happy is the man who is fully persuaded in his own mind, on the ground of his faith, as to what he approves, or decides to do.

23. The perfect past κατακέκριται is considered to be expressed by translating 'is already condemned.' The Apostle's argument seems to be, that he who is not fully persuaded in his mind as to whether he should eat or abstain from eating, and yet eats, is thereby condemned, because such conduct cannot proceed from faith, and "whatever is not from faith is sin." Faith is the antecedent of all virtue and all true knowledge. I cannot forbear expressing the opinion that what St Paul says in this Chapter respecting eating is figuratively applicable to *knowledge*. See Heb. v. 14 and xiii. 9.

CHAPTER XV. 1. The δέ is taken account of by making this verse begin a paragraph.

2. Τῷ πλησίον, '*his* neighbour,' not because the article has a pronominal force, but because πλησίον governs 'himself' understood.—Εἰς τὸ ἀγαθόν, ' with respect to what is good,' τὸ ἀγαθὸν being taken in a general sense. In an exhortation to do what pleases a neighbour, the limitation 'as to what is good' appears to be required, because the act would, otherwise, not be for his "edification." That εἰς may be translated 'with respect to' appears from the instances of its use in Eph. v. 32 and Heb. vii. 14.

3. Τῶν ὀνειδιζόντων σε, 'of them that reproach thee,' the present tense

indicating the applicability of this saying to the case of any one who is reproached.

4. In this passage two sources of hope are referred to, one being patience, which has already in v. 3, 4 been declared to be antecedent to hope, and the other, consolation, or comfort, derived from the Scriptures. The repetition of διὰ before παρακλήσεως shews that 'patience' is spoken of as a source distinct from 'comfort of the Scriptures.' The article before ὑπομονῆς may be considered to be abstract, just as in the instance in the next verse, and so may also that before παρακλήσεως, the species of the comfort being expressed by the addition 'of, or from the Scriptures.' 'There appears to be no reason for translating τὴν ἐλπίδα 'our hope,' as is done by the "Five Clergymen."

6. The article in τὸν θεὸν καὶ πατέρα is used just as in the simple appellation τὸν θεόν, but so as to refer both to θεόν and πατέρα. The full meaning is, 'the Being who is God and who is also Father of our Lord Jesus Christ.' It would, therefore, be incorrect to translate 'the God and Father, &c.,' because 'the God of our Lord Jesus Christ' is not expressed by the Greek. Neither would it be correct to translate 'God and the Father, &c.,' because this would not necessarily signify, as the original does, identity of person. The right translation into English is, therefore, that of the A. V., viz. 'God, even the Father,' which I have adopted, only omitting the word 'even.'

8. Γεγενῆσθαι, 'has become,' the weight of MSS. being rather more in favour of this reading than of γενέσθαι.—ὑπὲρ ἀληθείας θεοῦ, 'because of God's truth,' the next clause, 'to confirm the promises made to the fathers,' pointing to this rendering of the preposition. Also it seems that the Apostle intended ὑπὲρ to be taken in the same sense here as in the expression ὑπὲρ ἐλέους in the next verse, which plainly means 'because of mercy.'—Τὰς ἐπαγγελίας τῶν πατέρων, promises pertaining to the fathers only as being first delivered to them. The expression might, therefore, be taken in the general sense of 'antecedent promises,' the mention of 'the fathers' merely indicating the antecedence. This sense is, however, involved in the translation, 'the promises made to the fathers.'

9. Ὑπὲρ ἐλέους, literally 'because of mercy.' But the parallelism of this and the preceding expression, ὑπὲρ ἀληθείας θεοῦ, justifies translating 'because of his mercy.'—In the Septuagint ἐξομολογέομαι is frequently used to express 'giving of thanks.'

12. Ἐλπιοῦσιν, 'shall hope,' rather than 'shall trust,' on account of 'the God of hope' immediately following.

13. The δέ at the beginning of this verse only signifies what is differently indicated by punctuation.

14—16. In v. 14 δέ is transitional to another subject, and may, therefore, be translated 'now.'—In the same verse there is evidently a parallelism between καὶ αὐτὸς and καὶ αὐτοὶ which an exact translation ought to express. That this may be done by rendering the former 'on my part' and the other 'on your parts,' will, I think, appear from the following considerations. The Apostle, with the view of apologizing to the Romans for his boldness in venturing to write to them a letter containing instruction and exhortation, first assures them that it was not done from any doubt, on his part, as to their being, on their parts, "filled with knowledge and able to admonish one another;" then after intimating parenthetically that his motive was partly to put them in mind (see 2 Pet. iii. 1, 2), he gives as his main reason for writing to them, the grace he had received from God to be a minister of Jesus Christ to the Gentiles.—Ἱερουργοῦντα, 'performing a priest's office,' but here in a metaphorical sense.—Ἡ προσφορὰ τῶν ἐθνῶν, 'the offering consisting of believing Gentiles,' presented to God by the Apostle officiating as a priest. To avoid the ambiguity of 'the offering of the Gentiles,' I have translated 'the presenting of the Gentiles for an offering.'

17. Ἔχω οὖν καύχησιν, 'I have, therefore, boasting,' the ground of the boasting being the grace just before spoken of as being given to him by God.

18. The two negatives in this passage are equivalent to an affirmative. The proposed translation conforms in this respect to the original, inasmuch as ' other than those ' might be replaced by ' not those.'

19. Κύκλῳ, 'in a circuit,' this word being applicable to the course of the Apostle's travels from Jerusalem and Antioch, through Asia Minor, and thence through parts of Macedonia and Greece to Illyricum.—Τὸ εὐαγγέλιον may mean either preaching the gospel, or the gospel preached. The former meaning is applicable after πεπληρωκέναι.

20. Οὕτω δὲ φιλοτιμούμενον, 'thus striving,' that is, by taking this circuit. The δὲ is rendered by the punctuation. Φιλοτιμέομαι is used with respect to doing any thing with earnestness.

21. Οἷς οὐκ ἀνηγγέλη περὶ αὐτοῦ, 'to whom no announcement was made concerning him,' the verb being used impersonally.

22. Τὰ πολλά, 'for the most part,' that is, not wholly on that account.

23. From the Greek syntax it is obvious that the participle ἔχων is dependent on the nominative to ἐνεκοπτόμην. As this would not appear in English by strictly translating the participle, I have rendered it 'I have,' considering also that the full construction is 'I am having,' and that according to usage frequent in the Greek of the New Testament, 'I am' is omitted.—Ἐπιποθίαν ἔχων ἀπὸ πολλῶν ἐτῶν is 'having a desire of many years' continuance,' which might be turned into, ' having had for many years a desire.'

24. The text is followed as it stands in the Cod. Sin. and the majority of ancient MSS., in which ἐλεύσομαι πρὸς ὑμᾶς is omitted, and γὰρ is read after ἐλπίζω.—The literal rendering of the last clause of the verse is, 'if I should first have been partly filled with you.' The Vulgate has, ' si vobis primum ex parte fruitus fuero.'

27. Literally 'For they so thought good, and they are their debtors.' Εὐδόκησαν here is a repetition of the εὐδόκησαν at the beginning of v. 26; and the interpretation seems to be, for, at the same time that they (the Macedonians and Achaians) spontaneously thought good to do this, they are debtors to the saints at Jerusalem, the 'for' referring more especially to the latter reason. This view is conveyed by the proposed translation, which conforms closely to the original, inasmuch as 'besides that' may be considered to be the translation of καί.

28. Ἀπελεύσομαι, ' I will go,' not ' I will return,' as rendered in R. A.V.,

the preposition ἀπὸ signifying the intention of starting from Jerusalem to go by Rome to Spain.

31. Ἡ διακονία μου ἡ εἰς Ἰερουσαλήμ, 'the ministration I have for Jerusalem,' namely, that which he had just mentioned.

33. It seems inappropriate to introduce this short concluding prayer with the word 'now,' which, besides, is superfluous, the particle δέ being taken account of by the punctuation.

CHAPTER XVI. 1. Οὖσαν διάκονον, 'who is a deaconess,' this appellation being more distinctive than 'servant.'

2. Καὶ γὰρ αὕτη, 'for she, on her part,' analogous renderings of καὶ αὐτὸς and καὶ αὐτοὶ in xv. 14 having been already adopted.

3. Συνεργὸς is translated 'fellow-worker' in order, for the sake of distinction, to appropriate the word 'labor' to translating κοπιάω.

4. Ὑπέθηκαν, 'submitted,' better, perhaps, than 'laid down,' which is used to signify an actual surrender of life.—The clauses beginning with οἵτινες and ending with ἐθνῶν are interposed in a manner which in modern writing is usually indicated by *dashes*.

5. Τὸν ἀγαπητόν μου, 'my beloved, there being no more reason here for 'wellbeloved,' than in subsequent instances of the same expression.

7. 'Junias' rather than 'Junia,' the context favouring the supposition that this is the name of a man.

17. Παρὰ τὴν διδαχήν, 'in opposition to,' in order to render the preposition. 'Contrary to' might be an adjective agreeing with 'divisions and offences,' whereas it is the *causing* of divisions and offences which is contrary to the doctrine of Christ.

19. The γὰρ at the beginning of this verse introduces the Apostle's reasons for "beseeching" them.—Ἀφίκετο, 'gone abroad,' rather than 'come abroad.'—Εἰς τὸ ἀγαθὸν has already been translated 'with respect to what is good' in xv. 2. The present passage confirms that rendering. The A. V. has 'unto' for one εἰς and 'concerning' for the other. The R. A.V. gives 'unto' for both.

21. The translation 'saluteth you, and Lucius, &c.,' adopted in R. A.V., does not indicate that Lucius is not governed by 'saluteth.' To avoid the ambiguity I have employed the English phrase 'as do also.'

23. Ὁ ἀδελφός, 'a brother,' as rendered in A. V., the article only serving to convey the sense, 'one who is a brother.' R. A.V. has 'our brother,' although there is no pronoun in the Greek.

25—27. These verses contain a remarkable instance of interrupted construction analagous to that in xvi. 4. The interposed portion begins at κατὰ τὸ εὐαγγέλιον and ends with γνωρισθέντος, and may be regarded as a pendant to the words 'who is able to stablish you.' Without the interruption the sentence would stand thus: Τῷ δὲ δυναμένῳ ὑμᾶς στηρίξαι μόνῳ σοφῷ θεῷ διὰ Ἰησοῦ Χριστοῦ, which might be translated, 'To the only wise God, who is able to stablish you through Jesus Christ.' The construction of this sentence is not affected by the interposed passage, but the distribution of its parts relative to that passage can hardly be the same in English as that which is possible in Greek by reason of the terminal indications.

In the last clause of *v.* 27 the relative pronoun ᾧ presents considerable difficulty. I think, however, that its insertion is to be accounted for on the principle that it serves, after the long interruption of the construction by the interposed clauses, to revert to the Τῷ at the beginning of the sentence, and that since the construction is not incomplete without it (in the Codex B. ᾧ is omitted), it is indifferent, as far as regards that purpose, whether it be translated as a relative or a demonstrative pronoun. On these grounds ᾧ might be translated 'to Him.'

I have allowed the above remarks to stand, although eventually I judged it best to translate the passage quite strictly, and to preserve the order of the words in the original. My chief reason for so doing is, that I am much inclined to think that the apostle intends by this passage to *dedicate* the whole Epistle to God, and that τῷ δυναμένῳ is to be taken as signifying 'A service, or offering, to Him who is able, &c.' the dative case of itself admitting of this interpretation. In this way the relative pronoun ᾧ is accounted for.

CAMBRIDGE,
January, 1871.

LIST OF WORKS

PUBLISHED BY

MESSRS. DEIGHTON, BELL, & CO.

Agents to the University.

ALFORD (DEAN) The Greek Testament: with a critically revised Text; a Digest of Various Readings; Marginal References to Verbal and Idiomatic Usage; Prolegomena; and a Critical and Exegetical Commentary. For the use of Theological Students and Ministers. By HENRY ALFORD, D.D., Dean of Canterbury.

    Vol. I. *Sixth Edition*, containing the Four Gospels. 1*l*. 8*s*.

    Vol. II. *Fifth Edition*, containing the Acts of the Apostles, the Epistles to the Romans and Corinthians. 1*l*. 4*s*.

    Vol. III. *Fourth Edition*, containing the Epistle to the Galatians, Ephesians, Philippians, Colossians, Thessalonians,—to Timotheus, Titus, and Philemon. 18*s*.

    Vol. IV. Part I. *Fourth Edition*, containing the Epistle to the Hebrews, and the Catholic Epistles of St. James and St. Peter. 18*s*.

    Vol. IV. Part II. *Third Edition*, containing the Epistles of St. John and St. Jude, and the Revelation. 14*s*.

—————— The Greek Testament. With English Notes, intended for the Upper Forms of Schools and Pass-men at the Universities. By HENRY ALFORD, D.D. Abridged by BRADLEY H. ALFORD, M.A., late Scholar of Trinity College, Cambridge. One vol., crown 8vo. 10*s*. 6*d*.

—————— The New Testament for English Readers. Containing the Authorised Version, with additional corrections of Readings and Renderings; Marginal References; and a Critical and Explanatory Commentary. By HENRY ALFORD, D.D. In two volumes.

    Vol. I. Part I. Containing the First Three Gospels. *Second Edition*. 12*s*.

    Vol. I. Part II. Containing St. John and the Acts. *Second Edition*. 10*s*. 6*d*.

    Vol. II. Part I. Containing the Epistles of St. Paul. 16*s*.

    Vol. II. Part II. Containing the Epistle to the Hebrews, the Catholic Epistles, and the Revelation. 16*s*.

—————— Eastertide Sermons, preached before the University of Cambridge, on Four Sundays after Easter, 1866. By HENRY ALFORD, D.D. Small 8vo. 3*s*. 6*d*.

—————— A Plea for the Queen's English; Stray Notes on Speaking and Spelling. By HENRY ALFORD, D.D. Small 8vo. *Tenth Thousand*. 5*s*.

—————— Letters from Abroad. By HENRY ALFORD, D.D. Small 8vo. 7*s*. 6*d*.

LIST OF WORKS PUBLISHED BY

APOSTOLIC EPISTLES, A General Introduction to the, with a Table of St. Paul's Travels, and an Essay on the State after Death. *Second Edition, enlarged.* To which are added, A Few Words on the Athanasian Creed, on Justification by Faith, and on the Ninth and Seventeenth Articles of the Church of England. By a BISHOP'S CHAPLAIN. 8vo. 8s. 6d.

BARRETT (A. C.) Companion to the Greek Testament. For the use of Theological Students and the Upper Forms in Schools. By A. C. BARRETT, M.A., Caius College; Author of "A Treatise on Mechanics and Hydrostatics." *New Edition, enlarged and improved.* Fcap. 8vo. 5s.

> This volume will be found useful for all classes of Students who require a clear epitome of Biblical knowledge. It gives in a condensed form a large amount of information on the Text, Language, Geography, and Archæology; it discusses the alleged contradictions of the New Testament and the disputed quotations from the Old, and contains introductions to the separate books. It may be used by all intelligent students of the sacred volume; and has been found of great value to the students of Training Colleges in preparing for their examinations.

BEAMONT (W. J.) Cairo to Sinai and Sinai to Cairo. Being an Account of a Journey in the Desert of Arabia, November and December, 1860. By W. J. BEAMONT, M.A., formerly Fellow of Trinity College, Cambridge. With Maps and Illustrations. Fcap. 8vo. 5s.

—————— A Concise Grammar of the Arabic Language. Revised by SHEIKH ALI NADY EL BARRANY. By W. J. BEAMONT, M.A. Price 7s.

BLUNT (J. J.) Five Sermons preached before the University of Cambridge. The first Four in November, 1851, the Fifth on Thursday, March 8th, 1849, being the Hundred and Fiftieth Anniversary of the Society for Promoting Christian Knowledge. By J. J. BLUNT, B.D., formerly Lady Margaret Professor of Divinity, Cambridge. 8vo. 5s. 6d.

> CONTENTS: 1. Tests of the Truth of Revelation.—2. On Unfaithfulness to the Reformation.—3. On the Union of Church and State.—4. An Apology for the Prayer-Book.—5. Means and Method of National Reform.

BONNEY (T. G.) The Alpine Regions of Switzerland and the Neighbouring Countries. A Pedestrian's Notes on their Physical Features, Scenery, and Natural History. By T. G. BONNEY, B.D., F.G.S., &c., Fellow of St. John's College, Cambridge; Member of the Alpine Club. With Illustration by E. WHYMPER. 8vo., 12s. 6d.

—————— Death and Life in Nations and Men. Four Sermons preached before the University of Cambridge, in April, 1868. By T. G. BONNEY, B.D., Fellow of St. John's College. 8vo., price 3s. 6d.

BONWICKE (AMBROSE), Life of, by his father. Edited by JOHN E. B. MAYOR, M.A., Fellow of St. John's College, Cambridge. Small 8vo. 6s.

BROWNE (BP.) Messiah as Foretold and Expected. A Course of Sermons relating to the Messiah, as interpreted before the Coming of Christ. Preached before the University of Cambridge in the months of February and March, 1862. By the Right Reverend E. HAROLD BROWNE, D.D., Lord Bishop of Ely. 8vo. 4s.

BURN (R.) Rome and the Campagna. An Historical and Topographical Description of the Site, Buildings and Neighbourhood of Ancient Rome. By R. BURN, M.A., Fellow and Tutor of Trinity College, Cambridge. With Eighty-five Engravings by JEWITT, and Twenty-five Maps and Plans. 4to. cloth. £3. 3s.

The purpose of this work is to furnish students of the History and Literature of Rome with a description of the chief features of the site and buildings of the city during the regal, republican, and imperial eras, with a view especially to illustrate the writings of the principal Latin historians and poets. In the Introduction a sketch is given of the more prominent developments of ancient Roman architecture, and the illustrations they afford of Roman national character. Complete Indices are added of all the subjects discussed and of all passages quoted from classical authors, and also a list of modern works on Roman topography and antiquities.

CALVERLEY (C. S.) Verses and Translations. *Third Edit.* Fcap. 8vo. 5s.

——————— Translations into English and Latin. Crown 8vo. 7s. 6d.

——————— Theocritus translated into English Verse. Crown 8vo. 7s. 6d.

CAMBRIDGE University Calendar, 1870. 6s. 6d.

CAMPION (W. M.) Nature and Grace. Sermons preached in the Chapel Royal, Whitehall, in the year 1862-3-4. By WILLIAM MAGAN CAMPION, B.D., Fellow and Tutor of Queens' College, Cambridge, Rector of St. Botolph's, Cambridge, and one of her Majesty's Preachers at Whitehall. Small 8vo. 6s. 6d.

CANONESS (The). A Tale in verse of the time of the First French Revolution. Small 8vo. 5s.

CHEVALLIER (T.) Translation of the Epistles of Clement of Rome, Polycarp and Ignatius; and of the Apologies of Justin Martyr and Tertullian; with an Introduction and Brief Notes illustrative of the Ecclesiastical History of the First Two Centuries. By T. CHEVALLIER, B.D. *Second Edition.* 8vo. 12s.

COOPER (C. H. and THOMPSON). Athenae Cantabrigienses. By C. H. COOPER, F.S.A., and THOMPSON COOPER, F.S.A. Volume I. 1500—1585. 8vo. *cloth.* 18s. Volume II. 1586—1609. 18s.

DONALDSON (J. W.) The Theatre of the Greeks. A Treatise on the History and Exhibition of the Greek Drama: with various Supplements. By J. W. DONALDSON, D.D., formerly Fellow of Trinity College, Cambridge. *Seventh Edition,* revised, enlarged, and in part remodelled; with numerous illustrations from the best ancient authorities. 8vo. 14s.

——————— Classical Scholarship and Classical Learning considered with especial reference to Competitive Tests and University Teaching. A Practical Essay on Liberal Education. By J. W. DONALDSON, D.D. Crown 8vo. 5s.

ELLIS (ROBERT.) Enquiry into the Ancient Routes between Italy and Gaul; with an Examination of the Theory of Hannibal's Passage of the Alps by the Little St. Bernard. By ROBERT ELLIS, B.D., Fellow of St. John's College, Cambridge. 8vo. 6s.

ELLIS (A. A.) Bentleii Critica Sacra. Notes on the Greek and Latin Text of the New Testament, extracted from the Bentley MSS. in Trinity College Library. With the Abbé Rulotta's Collation of the Vatican MS., a specimen of Bentley's intended Edition, and an account of all his Collations. Edited, with the permission of the Masters and Seniors, by A. A. ELLIS, M.A., late Fellow of Trinity College, Cambridge. 8vo. 8s. 6d.

ELLIS (ROBERT LESLIE). The Mathematical and other Writings of ROBERT LESLIE ELLIS, M.A., formerly Fellow of Trinity College, Cambridge. Edited by WILLIAM WALTON, M.A., Trinity College, with a Biographical Memoir by the Very Reverend HARVEY GOODWIN, D.D., Dean of Ely. Portrait. 8vo. 16s.

EWALD (H.) Life of Jesus Christ. By H. EWALD. Edited by OCTAVIUS GLOVER, B.D., Emmanuel College, Cambridge. Crown 8vo. 9s.

────── The Prophet Isaiah. Chapters I—XXXIII. From the German of H. EWALD. By OCTAVIUS GLOVER, B.D. Crown 8vo. 6s.

FAMILY PRAYERS from or in the Style of the Liturgy; with Occasional Prayers and Thanksgiving. By Dr. HAMMOND, Bishop ANDREWS, and others. Crown 8vo. 3s.

FORSTER (CHARLES, B.D.) A New Plea for the Authenticity of the Text of the Three Heavenly Witnesses; or, Porson's Letters to Travis Eclectically Examined, and the External and Internal Evidences for 1 John v. 7 Eclectically Re-surveyed. By CHARLES FORSTER, B.D., Six-Preacher of Canterbury Cathedral, and Rector of Stisted, Essex; Author of "The Apostolic Authority of the Epistle to the Hebrews." 8vo. 10s. 6d.

FULLER (J. M.) Essay on the Authenticity of the Book of Daniel. By the Rev. J. M. FULLER, M.A., Fellow of St. John's College, Cambridge. 8vo. 6s.

FURIOSO, or, Passages from the Life of LUDWIG VON BEETHOVEN. From the German. Crown 8vo. 6s.

GLOVER (O.) A Short Treatise on Sin, based on the Work of Julius Müller. By O. GLOVER, B.D., Fellow of Emmanuel College, Cambridge. Crown 8vo. 3s. 6d.

────── Doctrine of the Person of Christ, an Historical Sketch. By OCTAVIUS GLOVER, B.D., Fellow of Emmanuel College, Cambridge. Crown 8vo. 3s.

"It is pleasant to welcome such a well-reasoned, thoughtful treatise as Mr. Glover's on the Doctrine of the Person of Christ. .... The whole book will be found most useful to students of Theology, especially when preparing for examination, the ten chapters being compact and well arranged."—*Church and State Review.*

GOODWIN (H., D.D., Lord Bishop of Carlisle). Doctrines and Difficulties of the Christian Religion contemplated from the Standing-point afforded by the Catholic Doctrine of the Being of our Lord Jesus Christ. Being the Hulsean Lectures for the year 1855. By H. GOODWIN, D.D. 8vo. 9s.

―――――― 'The Glory of the Only Begotten of the Father seen in the Manhood of Christ.' Being the Hulsean Lectures for the year 1856. By H. GOODWIN, D.D. 8vo. 7s. 6d.

―――――― Essays on the Pentateuch. By H. GOODWIN, D.D. Fcap. 8vo. 5s.

―――――― Parish Sermons. By H. GOODWIN, D.D. 1st Series. *Third Edition.* 12mo. 6s.

―――――― 2nd Series. *Third Edition.* 12mo. 6s.

―――――― 3rd Series. *Third Edition.* 12mo. 7s.

―――――― 4th Series, 12mo. 7s.

―――――― 5th Series. With Preface on Sermons and Sermon Writing. 7s.

―――――― Four Sermons preached before the University of Cambridge in February, 1869. I. Parties in the Church of England. II. Use and Abuse of Liberty in the Church of England. III. The Message of the Spirit to the Church of England. IV. Discussions concerning the Holy Communion in the Church of England. By H. GOODWIN, D.D. Small 8vo. 4s.

―――――― Four Sermons preached before the University of Cambridge, in the Season of Advent, 1858. By H. GOODWIN, D.D. 12mo. 3s. 6d.

―――――― Christ in the Wilderness. Four Sermons preached before the University of Cambridge in the month of February, 1855. By H. GOODWIN, D.D. 12mo. 4s.

―――――― Short Sermons at the Celebration of the Lord's Supper. By H. GOODWIN, D.D. *New Edition.* 12mo. 4s.

―――――― Lectures upon the Church Catechism. By H. GOODWIN, D.D. 12mo. 4s.

―――――― A Guide to the Parish Church. By H. GOODWIN, D.D. Price 1s. *sewed*; 1s. 6d. *cloth*.

―――――― Confirmation Day. Being a Book of Instruction for Young Persons how they ought to spend that solemn day, on which they renew the Vows of their Baptism, and are confirmed by the Bishop with prayer and the laying on of hands. By H. GOODWIN, D.D. *Eighth Thousand.* 2d., or 25 for 3s. 6d.

―――――― Plain Thoughts concerning the meaning of Holy Baptism. By H. GOODWIN, D.D. *Second Edition.* 2d., or 25 for 3s. 6d.

―――――― The Worthy Communicant; or, 'Who may come to the Supper of the Lord?' By H. GOODWIN, D.D. *Second Edition.* 2d., or 25 for 3s. 6d.

GOODWIN (Bishop). The Doom of Sin, and the Inspiration of the Bible. Two Sermons preached in Ely Cathedral: with some Prefatory Remarks upon the Oxford Declaration. By H. Goodwin, D.D. Fcap. 8vo. 1s. 6d.

——————— Hands, Head, and Heart; or the Christian Religion regarded Practically, Intellectually, and Devotionally. In Three Sermons preached before the University of Cambridge. By H. Goodwin, D.D. Fcap. 8vo. 2s. 6d.

——————— The Ministry of Christ in the Church of England. Four Sermons Preached before the University of Cambridge. I.—The Minister called. II.—The Minister as Prophet. III.—The Minister as Priest. IV.—The Minister Tried and Comforted. By H. Goodwin, D.D., Dean of Ely. Fcap. 8vo. 2s. 6d.

——————— The Appearing of Jesus Christ. A short Treatise by Symon Patrick, D.D., formerly Lord Bishop of Ely, now published for the first time from the Original MS. Edited by the Dean of Ely. 18mo. 3s.

——————— Commentaries on the Gospels, intended for the English Reader, and adapted either for Domestic or Private Use. By H. Goodwin, D.D. Crown 8vo.
S. MATTHEW, 12s.   S. MARK, 7s. 6d.   S. LUKE, 9s.

——————— On the Imitation of Christ. A New Translation. By the Dean of Ely. Third Edition. With fine Steel Engraving, after Guido, 5s.; without the Engraving, 3s. 6d. Cheap Edition, 1s. cloth, 6d. sewed.

GROTE (J.) Exploratio Philosophica. Rough Notes on Modern Intellectual Science. Part I. By J. Grote, B.D., formerly Professor of Moral Philosophy at Cambridge. 8vo. 9s.

——————— An Examination of the Utilitarian Philosophy, by John Grote, B.D., Fellow of Trinity College, and Professor of Moral Philosophy in the University of Cambridge. Edited by Joseph B. Mayor, M.A., late Fellow of St. John's College, Cambridge. 8vo. 12s.

HARDWICK (Archdeacon). History of the Articles of Religion. To which is added a series of Documents from A.D. 1536 to A.D. 1615. Together with illustrations from contemporary sources. By Charles Hardwick, B.D., late Archdeacon of Ely. *Second Edition, corrected and enlarged.* 8vo. 12s.

HUMPHRY (W. G.) An Historical and Explanatory Treatise on the Book of Common Prayer. By W. G. Humphry, B.D., late Fellow of Trinity College, Cambridge. *Third Edition, revised and enlarged.* Small post 8vo. 4s. 6d.

KENT's Commentary on International Law. Revised, with notes and Cases brought down to the present year. Edited by J. T. ABDY, LL.D., Regius Professor of Laws in the University of Cambridge, 8vo. 16s.

LAMB (J.) The Seven Words Spoken Against the Lord Jesus: or, an Investigation of the Motives which led His Contemporaries to reject Him. Being the Hulsean Lectures for the year 1860. By JOHN LAMB, M.A., Senior Fellow of Gonville and Caius College, and Minister of S. Edward's, Cambridge. 8vo. 5s. 6d.

LEAPINGWELL (G.) Manual of the Roman Civil Law, arranged according to the Syllabus of Dr. HALLIFAX. By G. LEAPINGWELL, LL.D. Designed for the use of Students in the Universities and Inns of Court. 8vo. 12s.

LEATHES (STANLEY). The Birthday of Christ, its Preparation, Message, and Witness. Three Sermons preached before the University of Cambridge, in December, 1865. By STANLEY LEATHES, M.A., Preacher and Assistant Minister, St. James's, Piccadilly, Professor of Hebrew, King's College, London. Fcap. 8vo. 2s.

LOBLEY (J.) The Church and the Churches in Southern India. A Review of the Portuguese Missions to that part of the world in the Sixteenth Century, with special reference to the Syrian Christians, and to modern Missionary efforts in the same quarter. The Maitland Prize Essay for 1870. By JOSE. :T ALBERT LOBLEY, M.A., Vicar of Hamer, Rochdale, formerly Feli˙ f Trinity College, Cambridge. 8vo. 4s.

MACKENZIE (BISHOP), Memoir of the la·ʿ. By the DEAN OF ELY. With Maps, Illustrations, and ar ·. ¡ᴛᵣᵥed Portrait from a painting by G. RICHMOND. Dedicated by .· ⁻ıssion to the Lord Bishop of Oxford. *Second Edition.* Small 8vo. 6s.

The Large Paper Edition may still be had, price 10s. 6d.

MACMICHAEL (W. F.) The Oxford and Cambridge Boat Races. A Chronicle of the Contests on the Thames in which University Crews have borne a part from A.D. 1829 to A.D. 1869. Compiled from the University Club Books and other Contemporary and Authentic Records, with Maps of the Racing Courses, Index of Names, and an Introduction on Rowing and its value as an Art and Recreation. By W. F. MACMICHAEL, B.A., Downing College, Secretary C. U. B. C. Fcap. 8vo. 6s.

MASKEW (T. R.) Annotations on the Acts of the Apostles. Original and selected. Designed principally for the use of Candidates for the Ordinary B.A. Degree, Students for Holy Orders, &c., with College and Senate-House Examination Papers. By T. R. MASKEW, M.A. *Second Edition,* enlarged. 12mo. 5s.

LIST OF WORKS PUBLISHED BY

MILL (W. H.) Observations on the attempted Application of Pantheistic Principles to the Theory and Historic Criticism of the Gospels. By W. H. MILL, D.D., formerly Regius Professor of Hebrew in the University of Cambridge. *Second Edition, with the Author's latest notes and additions.* Edited by his Son-in-Law, the Rev. B. WEBB, M.A. 8vo. 14s.

———— Lectures on the Catechism. Delivered in the Parish Church of Brasted, in the Diocese of Canterbury. By W. H. MILL, D.D. Edited by the Rev. B. WEBB, M.A. Fcap. 8vo. 6s. 6d.

———— Sermons preached in Lent 1845, and on several former occasions, before the University of Cambridge. By W. H. MILL, D.D. 8vo. 12s.

———— Four Sermons preached before the University on the Fifth of November and the three Sundays preceding Advent, in the year 1848. By W. H. MILL, D.D. 8vo. 5s. 6d.

———— An Analysis of the Exposition of the Creed, written by the Right Reverend Father in God, J. PEARSON, D.D., late Lord Bishop of Chester. Compiled, with some additional matter occasionally interspersed, for the use of Students of Bishop's College, Calcutta. By W. H. MILL, D.D. *Third Edition, revised and corrected.* 8vo. 5s.

MISSION LIFE among the Zulu-Kafirs. Memorials of HENRIETTA, Wife of the Rev. R. Robertson. Compiled chiefly from Letters and Journals written to the late Bishop Mackenzie and his Sisters. Edited by ANNE MACKENZIE. Small 8vo. 7s. 6d.

MORRIS (J.) Aids to Contentment. Selected by JOHN MORRIS, Editor of "The Book of Consolation." Crown 8vo. 5s.

MOULE (H. C. G.) Poems on Subjects selected from the Acts of the Apostles; with other Miscellaneous Pieces. By H. C. G. MOULE, M.A., Fellow of Trinity College, Cambridge. Fcap. 8vo. 4s.

NEALE (JOHN MASON.) Seatonian Poems. By J. M. NEALE, M.A., formerly Scholar of Trinity College. Fcap. 8vo. 6s.

NEWTON (SIR ISAAC) and Professor Cotes, Correspondence of, including Letters of other Eminent Men, now first published from the originals in the Library of Trinity College, Cambridge; together with an Appendix containing other unpublished Letters and Papers by Newton; with Notes, Synoptical View of the Philosopher's Life, and a variety of details illustrative of his history. Edited by the Rev. J. EDLESTON, M.A., Fellow of Trinity College, Cambridge. 8vo. 10s.

PALMER (E. H.) Oriental Mysticism. A Treatise on the Sufiistic and Unitarian Theosophy of the Persians. Compiled from Native Sources by E. H. PALMER, Fellow of St. John's College, Cambridge, Member of the Asiatic Society, and of the Société De Paris. Crown 8vo. 3s. 6d.

PEARSON (J. B.) The Divine Personality, being a Consideration of the Arguments to prove that the Author of Nature is a Being endued with liberty and choice. The Burney Prize Essay for 1864. By J. B. PEARSON, B.A., Fellow of St. John's College. 8vo. 1s. 6d.

PEROWNE (J. J. S.) Immortality. Four Sermons preached before the University of Cambridge. Being the Hulsean Lectures for 1868. By J. J. S. PEROWNE, B.D., Vice-Principal and Professor of Hebrew in St. David's College, Lampeter. 8vo. 7s. 6d.

PEROWNE (E. H.) The Godhead of Jesus; being the Hulsean Lectures for 1866; to which are added Two Sermons preached before the University of Cambridge on Good Friday and Easter Day, 1866. By E. H. PEROWNE, B.D., Fellow and Tutor of Corpus Christi College, Hulsean Lecturer, formerly one of her Majesty's Preachers at the Chapel Royal, Whitehall. 8vo. 5s.

PIEROTTI (ERMETE). Jerusalem Explored: being a Description of the Ancient and Modern City, with upwards of One Hundred Illustrations, consisting of Views, Ground-plans, and Sections. By ERMETE PIEROTTI, Doctor of Mathematics, Captain of the Corps of Engineers in the army of Sardinia, Architect-Engineer to his Excellency Sooraya Pasha of Jerusalem, and Architect of the Holy Land. Translated and edited by T. G. BONNEY, B.D., St. John's College. 2 vols. imperial 4to. 5l. 5s.

——— The Customs and Traditions of Palestine Compared with the Bible, from Observations made during a Residence of Eight Years. By Dr. ERMETE PIEROTTI, Author of "Jerusalem Explored." Translated and edited by T. G. BONNEY, B.D., St. John's College. 8vo. 9s.

PHILLIPS (GEO.) Short Sermons on Old Testament Messianic Texts, preached in the Chapel of Queens' College, Cambridge. By GEO. PHILLIPS, D.D., President of the College. 8vo. 5s.

——— A Syriac Grammar. By the Rev. G. PHILLIPS, D.D., President of Queens' College. *Third Edition, revised and enlarged.* 8vo. 7s. 6d.

PRITCHARD (C.) Analogies in the Progress of Nature and Grace. Four Sermons preached before the University of Cambridge, being the Hulsean Lectures for 1867; to which are added Two Sermons preached before the British Association. By C. PRITCHARD, M.A., President of the Royal Astronomical Society, late Fellow of S. John's College. 8vo. 7s. 6d.

PRYME (G.) Autobiographic Recollections of George Pryme, Esq., M.A., sometime Fellow of Trinity College, Professor of Political Economy in the University of Cambridge, and M.P. for the Borough. Edited by his Daughter. 8vo. 12s.

PSALTER (The) or Psalms of David in English Verse. With Preface and Notes. By a Member of the University of Cambridge. Dedicated by permission to the Lord Bishop of Ely, and the Reverend the Professors of Divinity in that University. 5s.

SCHOLEFIELD (PROF.) Hints for some Improvements in the Authorised Version of the New Testament. By J. SCHOLEFIELD, M.A., formerly Professor of Greek in the University of Cambridge. *Fourth Edition.* Fcap. 8vo. 4s.

SCOTT (G. G.) The Argument for the Intellectual Character of the First Cause as it is Affected by the more Recent Investigations of Physical Science. Being the Burney Prize Essay for the year 'CIƆIƆCCCLXVIII. By GEORGE GILBERT SCOTT, jun., B.A., F.S.A., of Jesus College, Cambridge. Crown 8vo. 2s. 6d.

10   LIST OF WORKS PUBLISHED BY

SCRIVENER (F. H.) Plain Introduction to the Criticism of the New Testament. With 40 Facsimiles from Ancient Manuscripts. For the Use of Biblical Students. By F. H. SCRIVENER, M.A., Trinity College, Cambridge. 8vo. 15s.

————— Codex Bezæ Cantabrigiensis. Edited, with Prolegomena, Notes, and Facsimiles. By F. H. SCRIVENER, M.A. 4to. 26s.

————— A Full Collation of the Codex Sinaiticus with the Received Text of the New Testament; to which is prefixed a Critical Introduction. By F. H. SCRIVENER, M.A. *Second Edition, revised.* Fcap. 8vo. 5s.

"Mr. Scrivener has now placed the results of Tischendorf's discovery within the reach of all in a charming little volume, which ought to form a companion to the Greek Testament in the Library of every Biblical student."—*Reader.*

————— An Exact Transcript of the CODEX AUGIENSIS, Græco-Latina Manuscript in Uncial Letters of S. Paul's Epistles, preserved in the Library of Trinity College, Cambridge. To which is added a Full Collation of Fifty Manuscripts containing various portions of the Greek New Testament deposited in English Libraries: with a full Critical Introduction. By F. H. SCRIVENER, M.A. Royal 8vo. 26s.

The CRITICAL INTRODUCTION *is issued separately, price* 5s.

————— Novum Testamentum Græcum, Textus Stephanici, 1550. Accedunt variæ lectiones editionem Bezæ, Elzeviri, Lachmanni, Tischendorfii, et Tregellesii. Curante F. H. SCRIVENER, M.A. 16mo. 4s. 6d.

An Edition on Writing-paper for Notes. 4to. *half-bound.* 12s.

SELWYN (PROFESSOR). Excerpta ex reliquiis Versionum, Aquilæ, Symmachi, Theodotionis, a Montefalconio aliisque collecta. GENESIS. Edidit GUL. SELWYN, S.T.B. 8vo. 1s.

————— Notæ Criticæ in Versionem Septuagintaviralem. EXODUS, Cap. I.—XXIV. Curante GUL. SELWYN, S.T.B. 8vo. 3s. 6d.

————— Notæ Criticæ in Versionem Septuagintaviralem. Liber NUMERORUM. Curante GUL. SELWYN, S.T.B.. 8vo. 4s. 6d.

————— Notæ Criticæ in Versionem Septuagintaviralem. Liber DEUTERONOMII. Curante GUL. SELWYN, S.T.B. 8vo. 4s. 6d.

————— Origenis Contra Celsum. Liber I. Curante GUL. SELWYN, S.T.B. 8vo. 3s. 6d.

————— Testimonia Patrum in Veteres Interpretes, Septuaginta, Aquilam, Symmachum, Theodotionem, a Montefalconio aliisque collecta paucis Additis. Edidit GUL. SELWYN, S.T.B. 8vo. 6d.

————— Horæ Hebraicæ. Critical and Expository Observations on the Prophecy of Messiah in Isaiah, Chapter IX., and on other Passages of Holy Scripture. By W. SELWYN, D.D., Lady Margaret's Reader in Theology. *Revised Edition, with Continuation.* 8s.

SELWYN (PROFESSOR). Waterloo. A Lay of Jubilee for June 18, A.D. 1815. *Second Edition.* 3s.

——— Winfrid, afterwards called Boniface. A.D. 680—755. Fcp. 4to. 2s.

SEELEY (H. G.) Index to the Fossil Remains of Aves, Ornithosauria, and Reptilia, from the Secondary System of Strata, arranged in the Woodwardian Museum of the University of Cambridge. By HARRY GOVIER SEELEY, of St. John's College, Cambridge. With a Prefatory Notice by the Rev. ADAM SEDGWICK, LL.D., F.R.S., Woodwardian Professor and Senior Fellow of Trinity College, Cambridge. 8vo. 2s. 6d.

——— Ornithosauria, an Elementary Study of the Bones of Pterodactyles, made from Fossil Remains found in the Cambridge Upper Greensand, and Arranged in the Woodwardian Museum of the University of Cambridge. By HARRY GOVIER SEELEY, of St. John's College, Cambridge. 8vo. 3s. 6d.

SINKER (R.) The Characteristic Differences between the Books of the New Testament and the immediately preceding Jewish, and the immediately succeeding Christian Literature, considered as an evidence of the Divine Authority of the New Testament. By R. SINKER, M.A., Chaplain of Trinity College, and late Crosse and Tyrwhitt University Scholar. Small 8vo. 3s. 6d.

——— Testamenta XII Patriarcharum; ad fidem Codicis Cantabrigiensis edita: accedunt Lectiones Cod. Oxoniensis. The Testaments of the XII Patriarchs: an attempt to estimate their Historic and Dogmatic Worth. By R. SINKER, M.A. Small 8vo. 7s. 6d.

STUDENT'S GUIDE (The) to the University of Cambridge. *Second Edition, revised and corrected in accordance with the recent regulations.* Fcap. 8vo. 5s.

    CONTENTS: Introduction, by J. R. SEELEY, M.A.—On University Expenses, by the Rev. H. LATHAM, M.A.—On the Choice of a College, by J. R. SEELEY, M.A.—On the Course of Reading for the Classical Tripos, by the Rev. R. BURN, M.A.—On the Course of Reading for the Mathematical Tripos, by the Rev. W. M. CAMPION, B.D.—On the Course of Reading for the Moral Sciences Tripos, by the Rev. J. B. MAYOR, M.A.—On the Course of Reading for the Natural Sciences Tripos, by Professor LIVEING, M.A.—On Law Studies and Law Degrees, by Professor J. T. ABDY, LL.D.—On the Ordinary B.A. Degree, by the Rev. J. R. LUMBY, M.A.—Medical Study and Degrees, by G. M. HUMPHRY, M.D.—On Theological Examinations, by Professor E. HAROLD BROWNE, B.D.—Examinations for the Civil Service of India, by the Rev. H. LATHAM, M.A.—Local Examinations of the University, by H. J. ROBY, M.A.—Diplomatic Service.—Detailed Account of the several Colleges.

TAYLOR (C.) The Gospel in the Law. A Critical Examination of the Citations from the Old Testament in the New. By CHARLES TAYLOR, M.A., Fellow of St. John's College. 8vo. 12s.

TERTULLIANI Liber Apologeticus. The Apology of Tertullian. With English Notes and a Preface, intended as an Introduction to the Study of Patristical and Ecclesiastical Latinity. By H. A. WOODHAM, LL.D. *Second Edition.* 8vo. 8s. 6d.

12 WORKS PUBLISHED BY DEIGHTON, BELL, & CO.

TODD (J. F.) The Apostle Paul and the Christian Church of Philippi. An Exposition Critical and Practical of the Sixteenth Chapter of the Acts of the Apostles and of the Epistles to the Philippians. By the late J. F. TODD, M.A., Trinity College, Cambridge. 8vo. 9s.

TREVELYAN (G. O.) The Ladies in Parliament, and other Pieces. Republished with Additions and Annotations. By G. O. TREVELYAN, late Scholar of Trinity College, Cambridge. 6s. 6d.

CONTENTS:—The Ladies in Parliament—Horace at Athens—The Cambridge Dionysia—The Dawk Bungalow—A Holiday among some Old Friends.

WIESELER's Chronological Synopsis of the Four Gospels. Translated by E. VENABLES, M.A., Canon of Lincoln, Examining Chaplain to the Bishop of London. 8vo. 13s.

WHEWELL (Dr.) Elements of Morality, including Polity. By W. WHEWELL, D.D., formerly Master of Trinity College, Cambridge. *Fourth Edition*, in 1 vol. 8vo. 15s.

—————— Lectures on the History of Moral Philosophy in England. By the Rev. W. WHEWELL, D.D. *New and Improved Edition, with additional Lectures.* Crown 8vo. 8s.

The Additional Lectures are printed separately in Octavo for the convenience of those who have purchased the former Edition. 3s. 6d.

—————— Astronomy and General Physics considered with reference to Natural Theology (Bridgewater Treatise). By W. WHEWELL, D D. *New Edition*, small 8vo. (Uniform with the Aldine.) 5s.

—————— Sermons preached in the Chapel of Trinity College, Cambridge. By W. WHEWELL, D.D. 8vo. 10s. 6d.

—————— Butler's Three Sermons on Human Nature, and Dissertation on Virtue. Edited by W. WHEWELL, D.D. With a Preface and a Syllabus of the Work. *Fourth and Cheaper Edition*. Fcap. 8vo. 2s. 6d.

WILLIS (R.) The Architectural History of Glastonbury Abbey. By R. WILLIS, M.A., F.R.S., Jacksonian Professor. With Illustrations. 8vo. 7s. 6d.

WILLIAMS (ROWLAND). Rational Godliness. After the Mind of Christ and the Written Voices of the Church. By ROWLAND WILLIAMS, D.D., Professor of Hebrew at Lampeter. Crn. 8vo. 10s. 6d.

—————— Paraméswara-jnyána-goshthi. A Dialogue of the Knowledge of the Supreme Lord, in which are compared the claims of Christianity and Hinduism, and various questions of Indian Religion and Literature fairly discussed. By ROWLAND WILLIAMS, D.D. 8vo. 12s.

WRATISLAW (A. H.) Notes and Dissertations, principally on Difficulties in the Scriptures of the New Covenant. By A. H. WRATISLAW, M.A., Head Master of Bury St. Edmund's School, late Fellow of Christ's College, Cambridge. 8vo. 7s. 6d.

CAMBRIDGE:—PRINTED BY JONATHAN PALMER.

www.ingramcontent.com/pod-product-compliance
Lightning Source LLC
Chambersburg PA
CBHW031405160426
43196CB00007B/909